kid chef
Bakes FOR THE
Holidays

kid chef Bakes FOR THE Holidays

THE KIDS' COOKBOOK FOR YEAR-ROUND CELEBRATIONS

Kristy Richardson

Photography by Elysa Weitala

ROCKRIDGE PRESS

For general information on our other products and services or to obtain technical support, please contact our Customer Care Department within the United States at (866) 744-2665, or outside the United States at (510) 253-0500.

Rockridge Press publishes its books in a variety of electronic and print formats. Some content that appears in print may not be available in electronic books, and vice versa.

TRADEMARKS: Rockridge Press and the Rockridge Press logo are trademarks or registered trademarks of Callisto Media Inc. and/or its affiliates, in the United States and other countries, and may not be used without written permission. All other trademarks are the property of their respective owners. Rockridge Press is not associated with any product or vendor mentioned in this book.

Interior and Cover Designer: Lisa Forde

Art Producer: Megan Baggott

Editors: Gleni Bartels, Bridget Fitzgerald

Production Editor: Mia Moran

Photography © 2020 Elysa Weitala. Food styling by Victoria Woollard, except page 15-16: Hélène Dujardin; page 23: Tara Donne

Author photo courtesy of Jemma-D Photography

ISBN: Print 978-1-64739-295-6
eBook 978-1-64739-296-3

R0

TO MY HUSBAND, NOEL,
for believing and loving me
every step of the way.

TO MY DAUGHTER, HAILEY,
for bringing joy to this book
and the kitchen.

CONTENTS

Introduction **x**

1: **Baking & Celebrating** 1

2: **Spring** 27

28
Lemonade
Bunny Thumbprint
Cookies

30
Easter Chick
Surprise!
Cupcakes

33
April Fools'
Tostada
Cookies

36
Gooey Passover
Double-Chocolate
Flourless Cookies

39
Raspberry and
Cream Cheese
Cupcakes

41
Sweet Orange
Hamantaschen
(Hat) Cookies

43
Ultimate Fiesta
Chocolate
Churro Cups

46
Blooming
Brownies

49
Eid Moon
Cookies

52
"You're a Smart
Cookie" Graduation
Cookies

3: **Summer** 55

56
Ultimate
Memorial Day
Pound Cake

59
Red, White,
and Blue Emoji
Cupcakes

61
Mermaid
Brownie
Pops

63
Camping
Party S'mores
Cookies

65
Shark
Attack
Cheesecakes

68
Brownie
à la Mode
Cupcakes

71
World Series
All-Star
Pull-Apart Cake

73
Watermelon
Pizza Cookie
Cake

75
Cool Strawberry and
Chocolate
Icebox Cake

77
Bursting
Blueberry Mini
Galettes (Pies!)

4: **Fall** 81

82
Spooky Ghost
Double-Chocolate
Cupcakes

86
Trick-or-Treat
Candy Overload
Brownies

88
Pumpkin Pie
Dumplings

91
Candy
Corn Magic
Cookies

92
Day of the Dead
Sugar Skull
Cookies

95
Fudgy
Diwali Chocolate
Burfi

97
Apple
Crisp Pizza
Party

100
Ooey-Gooey Maple-
Cinnamon French
Toast Muffins

102
Caramel Apple
Blondies

104
Changing
Leaves
Snickerdoodles

5: **Winter** 109

110
Chewy Cranberry,
Oatmeal, and
White Chocolate
Chip Cookies

112
Sweet Orange and
White Chocolate
Cookies

115
Stained
Glass Cookie
Ornaments

118
Chocolate Chip
and Almond Spanish
Polvorones

120
The Biggest Cinnamon-
Sugar Christmas Donut
Ever

122
Christmas Cutout
Cookies

125
Chocolate-
Peppermint
Crinkle Cookies

130
Chocolate-
Cinnamon Rugelach
Cookies

135
Lunar
New Year Walnut
Cookies

127
Let It
Snow! Snowman
Cake

132
Super Bowl
Football Field
Cookie Bars

137
Raspberry
Sweetheart
Rolls

6: **All Year Round** 141

143
Choco-Vanilla
Birthday Cake

148
School Spirit
Sprinkle Cookies

155
Caramel and
Pretzel Cookies

146
"Whoopie!
Thanks for Being
My Teacher" Pies

150
Bake Sale
Chocolate Chip
Shortbread Cookies

158
Nuts about
You Anniversary
Cookies

151
Feeling Prickly
Cactus Cupcakes

161
Peanut Butter
and Pumpkin
Pup Cookies

Measurement Conversions **163**

Index **164**

INTRODUCTION

Hi, I'm Kristy, and I'm so excited for us to bake together! I'm a mom of an eight-year-old girl, and we both love to spend time in the kitchen baking and cooking.

Growing up, baking at the holidays was a time for gathering in the kitchen. Every year in the winter, my mom would make tins full of cookies and chocolate-dipped sweets to share with family and friends. I'll never forget the year my mother surprised my dad with his favorite whoopie pies for his birthday. I've never seen his eyes so big!

As a grown-up, I started making baked goods with my husband as gifts for people at work or for parties. My husband also grew up baking with his mom. He's brought some of her recipes to our family, and I know she'd be proud to see us make her creations together.

Whether it's funny cupcakes for Halloween or sweet winter cookies, I love how our homemade treats make people smile. There is a little extra love and appreciation when someone takes the time to make you something from scratch—and it often tastes better, too!

The family baking trend continues, as my kid loves to bake, too. Every time she bakes or cooks, she becomes a little more confident in the kitchen, and you will, too! The best part is the big smile on her face when she's decorating or sharing treats with her family and friends, especially when it's time to celebrate.

While it was super hard for her to pick, her favorite recipes to make are the Let It Snow! Snowman Cake (page 127) and the Day of the Dead Sugar Skull Cookies (page 92), both of which she had fun decorating in creative ways. Her favorite recipe to eat is the "Whoopie! Thanks for Being My Teacher" Pies (page 146), though the Cool Strawberry and Chocolate Icebox Cake (page 75) is a close second!

In this book I'm sharing some of my favorite sweets and treats. This book is set up by season, so it's easy to flip through and find tasty treats that sound good now, no matter what time of year it is. Decorated cookies and treats aren't just for Christmas or Hanukkah—there are so many holidays to celebrate, and this book has tons of baking projects for holidays all year round.

You also may find some treats for some holidays that you aren't familiar with. If you've never celebrated (or heard of!) that holiday before, look it up to learn a little

more about it. You may be surprised when an amazing treat from a new holiday becomes your favorite!

The last chapter of the book contains recipes that are good for special events any time of the year, like treats to say thank you or give as birthday gifts.

Remember, just because a treat is listed for fall doesn't mean you can't make it for spring. A Valentine's Day treat is just as sweet as a gift for Mother's Day. The April Fools' sweet treat on page 33 is one of my favorites and also works for Cinco de Mayo or just Taco Tuesday! (Yes, you read that right—Taco Tuesday. You'll see why!)

I hope you have fun and make these recipes your own. Play with the decorations! Add your own ideas and change the colors. Find inspiration from what you find at your own grocery store. Swap out white chocolate chips for chocolate. Add some jelly beans for Easter or candy corn in fall.

Make the treats that make you smile. Find the treats that you want to eat and share with your family and friends and start there. When you bake something amazing, you kind of want to shout it from the rooftops! So let's get baking!

baking &
celebrating

Whether you're new to baking or just need a
refresher, this chapter is going to get you started on
all the basics that you'll need to bake like a pro!
Here you'll find all the tricks to making your favorite
sweet treats effortlessly! Use this chapter to cream
your butter perfectly every time, to know where you
can make smart substitutions, and to add the final
touches that make your treats shine at every holiday.

THE BEST OF BAKING

Baking for the holidays is such a fun way to spread joy with your family and friends. There is this magical moment when you pull out something fresh from the oven that is all warm and gooey. Your kitchen smells amazing, and you add the last special drizzle that makes a holiday extra sweet.

Baking also allows you to try new things and be creative! Surprise your family and friends with a themed treat they don't expect. A heart or a cozy pumpkin treat will make your eyes and taste buds sing. It's also so much fun to give baked treats as gifts, any time of year.

Be brave and add a few extra sprinkles. Try new things and make these recipes YOUR special recipe.

SOME GROUND RULES

Before we get started in the kitchen, let's chat about safety. All bakers (even the pros!) follow rules in the kitchen when working with sharp knives and hot ovens. Check out these ground rules that will help you make sure your sprinkles make it safely to your treats.

Read the recipe. Before you start baking, it's important to read the recipe from start to finish. Throughout the recipe are useful tips that can help keep you safe and help your treats be a success. You'll be sure you're not missing an important tool or ingredient halfway through. Plus, when you are up to your elbows in batter, it helps to know what is coming next!

Check in with an adult. Make sure a parent or another adult knows you will be baking. They may want to help you with certain steps or supervise to keep you safe. Adults can also help you if you run into a problem in the kitchen and you aren't sure what to do.

Be prepared. Good bakers start with checking themselves before they start baking. Think of this like you are a superhero changing into your uniform, getting ready to do your job. These steps will make sure you are ready to start baking.
- Wash and dry your hands.
- Pull back your hair in a hair tie or under a hat.
- Protect your clothes with an apron.

Prepare your ingredients. It's time to gather all the ingredients and look for anything you can prep ahead.

- Do you need to soften the butter or cream cheese?
- Can you chop an ingredient ahead of time?
- Can you premeasure or prewash some of your ingredients?
- Do you have all the ingredients in the recipe?

Prepare your tools and check the time. Check your list of tools before you start your recipe.

- Make sure you have everything you need and can find your tools.
- Now is a great time to preheat the oven, lay parchment paper on baking sheets, or grease your pans.
- Check the timing on the recipe and make sure you have enough time for all the steps. Sometimes a recipe may call for chilling the dough in the refrigerator for a while, or even overnight! Make sure you know the time you'll need.

Play it safe. Paying attention to your surroundings is key in kitchen safety. If you're ever unsure, ask an adult for help, and be sure to:

- Watch out for hot pans.
- Be extra careful when the oven or mixer is on.
- Watch sharp knives!

Know some cleanup tricks. Make cleanup easier on yourself so baking is more fun.

- Clean as you go and you'll have much less to clean at the end. That means wiping down a surface right after you spill flour all over it (it happens to everyone) and putting used bowls and measuring tools in the sink or dishwasher right away.
- Fill your mixing bowl with warm water after the dough is gone. Add dirty cups or spoons for easier cleanup.
- Make sure you have enough room to prepare your recipe so you have fewer messes. While you're waiting for a next step, use the pause to wash a big bowl or put away ingredients you're done with. It will make life easier later, I promise.

BAKING TOOLS & EQUIPMENT

There are so many great kitchen gadgets out there, but how many do you really need? The good news is, often the same tools can help you make tons of different types of baked treats. Read the list, and check with your nearest adult in charge—does your kitchen have the basic gear? As you get more into baking, you can add more items as needed.

Baking Gear You Need

Use this list to find the must-have items you'll need for baking the treats in this book.

 Oven mitts/pot holders Thick oven mitts protect not only your hands but the tops of your arms, too. Extra pot holders are handy to put hot pans on top of.

 Spatula Silicone spatulas are great for mixing and scraping batter from your mixing bowl. I recommend all bakers have one. A thin metal spatula is handy for frosting cookies, and especially for cakes.

 Whisk Whisks whip air into your eggs, butter, and even the batter when needed. They can also help mix dry and wet ingredients so they blend together.

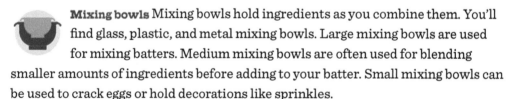 **Mixing bowls** Mixing bowls hold ingredients as you combine them. You'll find glass, plastic, and metal mixing bowls. Large mixing bowls are used for mixing batters. Medium mixing bowls are often used for blending smaller amounts of ingredients before adding to your batter. Small mixing bowls can be used to crack eggs or hold decorations like sprinkles.

Measuring cups/spoons Bakers need at least one full set of measuring cups and spoons to make sure you add the right amount of ingredients. I like to keep two sets of measuring cups and spoons in my kitchen—one set for wet ingredients and another for dry ingredients. This helps you measure more accurately, and different types of measuring cups work better for different ingredients. (Read more about wet versus dry ingredients on page 13.)

- Metal or plastic measuring cups work best for dry ingredients (such as flour and sugar). You can scoop into them and level them off with a butter knife to help measure dry powders more accurately.

- Glass or clear plastic measuring cups (like a 2-cup Pyrex measuring cup) work best for liquids. Set the cup on the counter and look at it from the side to see that the liquids are right at the line. Then you'll know you have the right amount.

 Baking pans & sheets There are so many different types of pans. Here's how to use them:

- Metal baking sheets are great for cookies.

- Metal muffin pans (also called cupcake pans) should be in every baker's kitchen and are used for many treats.

- Mini muffin pans make fun mini desserts. Most recipes you make with a muffin pan can be made mini, but watch the time. They will cook much faster!

- Round metal pans are good for layer cakes—you'll need two 8- or 9-inch cake pans.

- Square metal pans are great for brownies, helping keep them chewier than when they are baked in a glass pan (which can make them crisp up too fast).

- An 8-by-11-inch metal pan will make a great sheet cake or cookie bars.

- A glass pie pan is for crispy piecrusts and lets you see if it's burning right away.

- A metal Bundt pan (a round pan with a hole in the middle with bumpy "fluted" sides) is for cakes and is handy to have. These are sometimes confused with a metal tube pan, which is made of two pieces and used for lighter cakes like angel food cake.

Electric mixer Electric mixers are useful and often necessary for blending batters or whipping air into eggs. While a whisk also whips air, some techniques are harder to do by hand. (You wouldn't think stirring could cause your arm to get tired—but it can!) I recommend every baker have an electric hand mixer for blending.

Parchment paper or baking mats Parchment paper is needed in most recipes to help baked goods release easily from the pan. Silicone baking mats—great for lining baking sheets—are nice to have and are reusable, but they can't be cut to size for smaller or round pans.

WHAT SHOULD MY PAN BE MADE OF?

Metal pans leave desserts chewier and protect more delicate batters and doughs from burning as easily. Metal pans are perfect for cookies, brownies, and cakes. Many of the recipes in this book work well with metal pans.

Dark metal pans tend to cook a little crispier because they reflect more heat. Your dessert will brown faster and may need to cook for less time on or in a dark metal pan.

Glass pans work best for desserts you want to be crispy, such as piecrust. They hold on to heat longer but also don't heat up as quickly for faster-cooking desserts.

Silicone pans can be great for baking in fun shapes, because it is much easier to slide treats out of the pan. The sides of a silicone pan aren't sturdy, so remember to always place a silicone pan on a baking sheet to keep from spilling hot batter or dough. Treats also don't brown when baked in a silicone pan.

Baking Gear That's Nice to Have

Once you've got the basics of baking down, you might want to expand your baking gear. Here are a few items that are handy (but not necessary) for any baker to have.

 Cookie cutters Cookie cutters aren't needed in every recipe but are super helpful for making fun shapes.

 Cookie scoop These little scoops look like small ice cream scoops, and they aren't just for cookies. They can help you portion out dough quickly and evenly.

 Rolling pin A rolling pin is used mostly for rolling dough for cutout cookies or using as a mallet for making crumbs (on purpose!) Substitute a clean bottle with smooth sides in a pinch.

 Cooling racks Cooling racks help cookies, cupcakes, and cakes cool faster and more evenly. Many desserts can be transferred to a towel as they finish cooling instead, but it will take a little longer. If you're trying to cool something quickly to stop the cooking process, many baked goods can be placed in the refrigerator or freezer to speed things up.

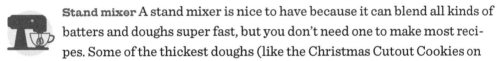 **Stand mixer** A stand mixer is nice to have because it can blend all kinds of batters and doughs super fast, but you don't need one to make most recipes. Some of the thickest doughs (like the Christmas Cutout Cookies on page 122) are great to make with a stand mixer. A hand mixer can also do the job but should not be used for sugar cookie doughs, as they are too heavy and might break your hand mixer. For those you can use a heavy wooden spoon instead.

OVEN SAFETY & TIPS

Ouch, that's hot! When using the oven, you must be extra careful. Here are a few quick tips to keep you safe:

- Check that nothing is on top of or inside the oven before turning it on.

- Use a dry oven mitt for moving pans in or out of the oven. (Water on your oven mitt means that the heat can go through the mitt and possibly burn you—ouch!)

- Be extra careful around the top and sides of the hot oven once it's on.

- If your oven has a stovetop on top, don't place items on top of the oven, other than a hot pan. Don't place anything on top of burners that have been on. Don't reach across hot burners.

- Alert anyone in the kitchen with you when you are opening the oven door. In restaurant kitchens, it's customary to yell out "Hot oven!" every time.

- Use the oven light to peek at your treats instead of opening the door. This also helps keep baking times accurate.

- Always turn the oven off when you are done baking.

- If you are unsure about something, ask an adult for help.

- If you do accidentally burn your finger, run it under cold water immediately. Then tell an adult.

THE HOLIDAY BAKER'S PANTRY

Every baker has ingredients they always need and can grab for a special recipe, items like flour, sugar, and powdered sugar. You're going to need those! Other items are nice to have for special treats, but you won't always need them. Check out the lists to plan your grocery run!

Must-Haves

Every baker needs a few important items in stock at all times. Here are some of the basics you're going to need over and over again!

Baking powder and baking soda These are used to make baked goods rise without yeast and also to offset acidity in baked goods. Keep a small container of each in the pantry. Be sure to check the expiration dates on these. Expired baking powder or baking soda could mean your baked good won't rise.

Chocolate chips Whether you're making Chewy Cranberry, Oatmeal, and White Chocolate Chip Cookies (page 110) or a delicious chocolate sauce (page 44), chocolate chips need to be on your grocery list! Semisweet is used the most often, but using different flavors of chips is an easy way to change up your cookies.

Eggs Eggs bind cakes, cookies, and other sweets together, making them rich and delicious.

Flour Flour is the base of most baked goods (except for desserts like the Gooey Passover Double-Chocolate Flourless Cookies on page 36). For most of the recipes in this book, you'll use all-purpose flour. A few recipes call for self-rising flour, which is a special type of flour with baking soda and salt already mixed in. You cannot swap regular all-purpose flour in place of self-rising flour—your treats will not rise.

Milk or heavy cream Many recipes require milk, heavy cream, or both. Read carefully so you have what you need!

Salt You might not think of salt when it comes to sweets and desserts, but you'll often use a little salt to bring out other flavors. Don't worry, it won't make anything taste salty.

Sprinkles Sprinkles add a touch of fun and holiday cheer. Have a few colors to choose from.

Sugar Granulated sugar, light brown sugar, and powdered sugar (also called confectioners' sugar) are all used very often in baked goods.

Unsalted butter Bakers use unsalted butter because it allows them to control the amount of salt in their recipes. It's important to have enough salt in your desserts to bring out the flavors, but not so much that it will make them taste salty.

Unsweetened cocoa powder Cocoa flavors all kinds of batters, especially brownies. For baking, use unsweetened cocoa, which is different from cocoa mix meant for hot chocolate.

Vanilla extract Good-quality vanilla makes baked goods sing. It's used as a base flavor in chocolate- and fruit-flavored desserts, too! Use real vanilla if you can, and skip bottles labeled "imitation." Pour vanilla carefully, as it can be an expensive ingredient. You don't want to waste any. If there are no nut allergies to worry about, almond extract can often be a substitute.

THE SCIENCE BEHIND THE BAKE

Baking isn't just fun—it's science, too. Mixing the wrong amounts of ingredients can change your perfect buttery baked treat into an accidental rock. Here are some ways our ingredients affect the finished product:

Butter Butter adds flavor. It also adds fat. Temperature is important with butter—too warm, and your baked goods will spread too fast. This can mess up the shapes of cutout cookies or just give you too-big treats with the wrong texture.

Baking soda and baking powder Baking soda and baking powder create a reaction both when you mix the dough and again when your treat is being baked, causing your batter to rise. These ingredients will also balance flavors in your recipe from items like cocoa, brown sugar, lemon, and buttermilk. But adding too much of either can make things taste dull or chalky.

Eggs Eggs add a richness, a little fat, and liquid to batters. Too many eggs, and the batter won't hold its shape. Egg whites on their own can be whipped into stiff peaks (like in the Gooey Passover Double-Chocolate Flourless Cookies on page 36) or brushed on top of baked goods to help them brown.

Liquids Liquids like milk and water can help powders like flour and sugar dissolve and blend.

Salt All the recipes in this book use unsalted butter. The amount of salt in salted butter affects flavor. While a little salt brings out the flavors of chocolate, caramel, and nuts, too much salt makes treats taste . . . well, salty!

Nice-to-Haves

These items are nice to have in your pantry and can help make your baked goods look beautiful and taste even better!

Birthday candles Keep a few candles on hand and you'll never need to make a dash to restock right before someone's birthday again!

Candy eyes You can make eyes with frosting, but candy eyes are an easy way to make faces come alive. You can often find these at craft stores in the baking section or even in the grocery store.

Candy melts Candy melts come in a rainbow of colors and can be melted down and drizzled over most recipes for a pop of color.

Colored chocolate candies Colored chocolate candies (like M&M's) are often used as decorations. Most of the time a small bag is enough!

Cream cheese Cream cheese is in some recipes, often in delicious frostings.

Food coloring (gel or liquid) Food coloring can be used to change the color of frostings and batters. Gel food coloring is preferred by most bakers and makes brighter colors. Liquid food coloring can be used in most treats, but your colors will be less vibrant and you will use more food coloring.

Marshmallows Marshmallows can add flavor to cookies or be used to decorate the tops of your treats.

Meringue powder This powder is a mix of dried egg whites and cream of tartar used to make a royal icing. You can find it at large craft or grocery stores in the baking section or online. (My favorite brand is Wilton's.) Any cookie recipes made with royal icing can also be frosted with buttercream, but you won't be able to get as detailed.

Seasonal candy and decorations You can find so many candies and toppings to choose from at the grocery store, at the craft store, or even at a party store—whether it's snowflake sprinkles for winter, chocolate spiders for Halloween, or candy corn in Christmas colors. (I've seen it!) You can find simple and wild toppers. Sometimes it helps to let your trip to the store inspire your decorations.

SKILLS TO MASTER

Every expert baker started as a beginner. This chapter will teach you important baking skills like how to measure ingredients, chop just right, and cream the perfect frosting. As discussed in the sidebar on page 11, ingredients—and their amounts—are super important. For example, if you don't measure the right amount of baking soda, your treats can go from gooey and delicious to dry and powdery—yuck! Check out the tips below to keep it from happening to you.

Measuring

Let's talk about measuring. In this book we use imperial measurements, which means cups and tablespoons. Some bakers measure ingredients by weight to get more exact measurements. While we don't have to be perfect down to the last grain of salt, measuring accurately will help your treats come out delicious every time.

WET INGREDIENTS

Many wet ingredients can be measured with measuring cups or spoons. Wet ingredient measuring tools are often clear glass with a handle and a spout for pouring, with the measurements marked on the side.

- Make sure you measure right up to the marking so you have enough liquid.

- Eggs can vary in size. Recipes in this book call for large eggs, but not all eggs are the same. If your eggs are especially small, try adding an extra tablespoon of egg from an additional egg (whip it with a fork in a small bowl first) to your recipe if needed.

- Some brands of dry ingredients can suck up more liquid than expected! If your dough looks too dry to roll or shape, try adding water—a tablespoon at a time—until the dough looks right. In recipes with trickier doughs, I'll often explain how the dough should feel or look so you'll know if you're on the right track.

DRY INGREDIENTS

Dry ingredients are very easy to measure, even using the same measuring cup! These cups are often plastic or metal and come in a nested set. A cup of flour packed into the measuring cup tightly will be a very different measurement from a cup of flour spooned into the cup loosely, so always follow these guidelines.

- When measuring dry ingredients like flour and sugar, use a spoon to scoop from your bag into your measuring cup. Using the measuring cup to directly scoop dry ingredients that have lots of tiny pieces like flour or sugar will pack it too tightly in the cup and cause you to have too much.

- Be extra careful that you have the right-size spoon for measuring baking powder and baking soda. Grabbing a teaspoon instead of a tablespoon for these ingredients will ruin your batter or dough.

- Use the flat side of a butter knife to make sure your ingredient is level with your measuring cup. Keeping your measuring cup over the ingredient's container, start at one end of the cup and push your knife across the cup, removing any extra above the edge of the cup to level it off.

OTHER

Sticky ingredients like peanut butter, honey, or even yogurt can sometimes be hard to get out of your measuring cup. Spray the inside of your measuring cup or spoon with a very light coat of oil, and the ingredients will slide right out and into the mixing bowl.

If the recipe calls for chopping in the ingredient list, measure that ingredient *after* chopping. More chopped walnuts fit in a measuring cup than big walnut pieces.

Mixing

Certain words in baking mean different ways to mix and put together your doughs and batter. Below I'll explain them and help you understand what is happening to your ingredients.

BEATING & CREAMING

When you see the word **beat** in the recipe, it means that you need to mix this recipe fast. This is to combine all the ingredients and add a little air to your batter. You will also often see that you need to beat eggs—this breaks the yolk and mixes the yolk and the white together.

Usually you start by mixing the wet ingredients well, then adding the dry ingredients. When you mix the dry and wet ingredients together, start slowly and then speed up as the dry ingredients mix in more. If you beat a batter with dry ingredients too fast, be prepared for flour and sugar to fly everywhere! **Whipping** a batter is also pretty much the same as beating it. Use a whisk, silicone spatula, or spoon to beat, but for some recipes it is easier to use a hand mixer or stand mixer.

Creaming means you are taking an ingredient with lots of fat, like butter, and adding other ingredients like sugar to mix them together and increase the overall volume. Creaming should leave your butter (or other high-fat ingredients like shortening) light and fluffy. Creaming can be done by hand with a spatula or spoon or with a handheld mixer, or in a stand mixer with the paddle attachment.

Sometimes people think they can skip creaming the wet ingredients together and just throw all the ingredients in a bowl together. But stop! Don't do it! This will change the texture of your baked goods, and not in a good way. Sure, recipes can still work sometimes if you don't cream your ingredients. But for baked goods that are light, moist, smooth, buttery, and even crumbly in just the right way? You want to cream wet ingredients separately from mixing dry ingredients.

FOLDING & STIRRING

Stirring and folding are the easier types of mixing! When you are **stirring**, you're simply mixing until everything is combined. This is usually mixing dry ingredients into wet and making sure everything is mixed well.

Folding usually happens at the end of the recipe when you are adding something extra to the batter, like chocolate chips, nuts, or sprinkles. Folding in something at the end helps keep that item as a bigger piece. If a recipe tells you to "fold in" an ingredient, here's how you do it:

- Add the ingredient to the batter.

- Use a big spoon or spatula to pull the new ingredient into the batter gently. You may need to pull some of the batter or dough from the bottom over the ingredient you are folding in.

- Repeat a few times until the new ingredient is mixed throughout the bowl. This is like super-slow stirring and helps keep things like nuts and chocolate chips from falling apart when you add them. (Check out the Caramel and Pretzel Cookies, where we fold in bits of pretzel, on page 155.)

CUTTING IN

In some recipes you may see that an ingredient needs to be **cut in**. This is almost always talking about butter, sometimes shortening. When you cut in butter, you're adding small pieces of cold butter to flour. You're trying to keep the butter as cold as possible to keep it from spreading in your baked treat and to add flakiness to the texture. The small pieces will remain intact rather than fully mixing with the flour. Pros often do their cutting in by mixing with a pastry cutter. You can also do this by mixing butter into the dry ingredients with a fork, or even grating frozen butter and then mixing it into the flour. It is easier to cut butter into your flour if you cut the stick into smaller pieces first.

Cutting

Using sharp knives is part of being in the kitchen. Use these tips to help you use knives safely with the help of an adult.

KNIFE SKILLS

Always use a cutting board with your knife so you have a steady cutting surface. Keep the blade near your cutting board and always know where the knife is! When you pass a knife to someone, point the blade down and pass it by the handle. Younger chefs will start with a small knife meant for slicing small items, or even knives made of nylon that cut ingredients but not fingers. As you practice more, try bigger knives when an adult says it's OK.

Chop This means to cut something into rough but even chunks. Nuts and chocolate are both ingredients you chop. To chop, hold the handle of the knife in your writing hand with the blade facing down, and place your other hand out flat along the top of the blade (the sharp part of the blade will be facing down!) Move your writing hand up and down in a rocking motion to cut your ingredient. Keep your fingers flat and away from the sharp part of the blade.

Slice Slicing means to cut the ingredient into even pieces. You might slice a dough (like the Raspberry Sweetheart Rolls on page 137), fruit, or even candy. If you slice uneven pieces, your treats often will have some that are overcooked or underdone. To slice, hold the knife in your writing hand with the sharp part of the blade facing down. Hold the item you are slicing steady with your other hand. Keep your fingers away from the blade by keeping your hand in a claw shape, with fingertips tucked in. Line up your knife and move the knife down, carefully making one cut at a time.

Using a Grater

Shred or grate To shred or grate, you need to use a tool called a grater. A grater has small holes that shred ingredients into small, thin pieces. The bigger holes can be used for ingredients like cold butter, chocolate, or carrots. Press your ingredient with your writing hand against the grater and hold the grater steady with your nonwriting hand. Move the ingredient up and down along the grater to make shreds, keeping your fingertips back. They may not look it, but graters are seriously sharp!

Zest Zesting is done with citrus fruits like lemons and oranges. Use a grater to remove some of the outside of the fruit in tiny shreds. The smaller holes on a grater can work, or you can use a tool for zesting called a zester. These tiny shreds of fruit rind pack a lot of flavor (like in the Lemonade Bunny Thumbprint Cookies on page 28). When zesting, shred only the colorful part of the rind. Underneath the colorful rind is a white layer called the pith that has a bitter taste.

Frosting, Icing, and Glaze

There are many different options for frosting and icing to make your treats look amazing. It's the finishing touches that make your sweet treats pop! **Frosting** tends to be thicker and fluffier, like on the top of a cake. **Icing** tends to be thinner, sometimes even drippy. It is often used to decorate sugar cookies. A **glaze** is like an icing but even more liquid.

PIPING

Piping is when you take frosting (or even occasionally dough), put it in a bag, and push it out of a small hole to decorate, write, or add pretty details to treats.

Piping like a pro with gear You've likely seen frosting piped into all different kinds of fluffy shapes and textures. To do more complicated designs, you'll need some piping bags, metal tips in a variety of shapes, and a coupler, which attaches the tip to the bag. You can create all kinds of stars, flowers, lines, zigzags, and beautiful shapes. If you love to bake, I highly recommend you pick up a small, inexpensive set and start experimenting!

Piping like a pro—without gear! You don't need a piping set to get started. Rather than frost with a knife or spatula, put your frosting into a thick zip-top bag. I like to use a quart- or gallon-sized freezer bag, as they are stronger. Then snip a tiny part of the corner from the bag and squeeze your frosting out of the hole. The bigger you make that hole, the bigger your frosting will be when you squeeze it out of the bag.

- For smaller frosting details (like on my "You're a Smart Cookie" Graduation Cookies on page 52), cut a tiny hole and then test your line size on parchment paper. You can always make the hole bigger, but not smaller, so snip carefully.

- For bigger frosting swirls (like the frosting on top of the Spooky Ghost Double-Chocolate Cupcakes on page 82), cut a slightly larger hole. Start in the middle and build a little swirl of icing by pressing down lightly as you swirl from the inside out. Then build the height on the frosting by continuing to swirl while moving back toward the center and up. You can practice this on parchment paper and then pop that frosting right back into your bag to pipe your cupcakes (as long as it's a single-color frosting).

How to fill a piping bag the easy way Filling a bag full of frosting can get messy fast, whether it's a piping bag or a strong zip-top bag. You'll need a tall drinking glass (a glass that holds 16 to 24 ounces is perfect), a bag, and a frosting spatula or butter knife.

- Place the tip of the plastic bag down in the bottom of the glass.

- Fold the sides of the bag down over the outside of the glass, opening up the bag.

- Use your spatula or butter knife to fill the bag, gently pushing as much of the icing down into the glass while holding the glass stable with your other hand.

- Once full, pull the sides of the bag up. Push the icing down toward the tip, then twist the top of the bag until it's tight.

- While keeping the top twisted, snip a small hole in the tip of the bag. Start small— you can always cut the hole bigger if you need to, but you can't make it smaller. Happy decorating!

Other techniques I'll share a few other techniques with frosting in this book (like making scales with frosting on the Mermaid Brownie Pops on page 61), so keep your eyes out for more tips! You can also find all kinds of creative ways to pipe frosting online or in books from the library.

HIGH-ALTITUDE COOKING

Do you live at 5,000 feet or more above sea level? If you live in the mountains or higher up, it can affect how your treats bake and how they turn out.

WHY DOES BAKING CHANGE IN HIGHER ALTITUDES?

When you live at a higher altitude, the air pressure changes. Baked goods will rise faster, which causes them to cook a little faster, or they may dry out more. If you don't adjust your ingredients a little, baked goods can turn out denser, drier, or even fall in the middle. Baking is chemistry, so by adjusting the ingredients a bit, the recipes will still work.

All the recipes in this book are written and tested for regular sea level. Depending on how high up you are, you may have to adjust these a little more or less.

RECIPE ADJUSTMENTS FOR HIGH ALTITUDE

Living 5,000 feet up myself, I've learned a few tricks that have helped. Start with the bake time and baking powder—those are the easiest to adjust.

Watch bake time carefully. All treats will bake faster at higher altitude, so start checking on them a few minutes before the recipe says.

Reduce baking powder. For each teaspoon of baking powder, I reduce between ⅛ and ¼ teaspoon. This helps keep the treats from rising too fast and then collapsing.

Reduce sugar. Decrease your sugar by 1 to 2 tablespoons for every cup. This will help your treats maintain their structure and make them less likely to fall in when baking.

Increase liquids. For every cup of liquid in your recipe, add 2 to 4 tablespoons of liquid. I add egg (in recipes that have egg already) or water. Extra milk can throw off the recipe. Adding liquids helps because treats at high altitude dry out faster.

Increase your oven temperature by 25°F. This helps the treats cook and set a little faster. Check on them so they don't overcook.

TROUBLESHOOTING

Part of being a baker is learning from your mistakes. Here are a few issues that sometimes come up with baked treats and ways to fix them next time.

Too Thick or Too Dense

Sometimes cookies, brownies, or other baked goods just come out a bit less fluffy and a little too solid. Here are some things to watch for:

1. **Check expiration dates.** Baking soda and baking powder can both expire and then don't work quite right!

2. **The butter didn't cream enough.** Creaming the butter helps develop lightness and airiness. Your butter should get slightly lighter in color when creamed well.

3. **The dry ingredients were packed too tight.** Scoop with a spoon into your measuring cup and level your dry ingredients (see page 14) so you don't have too much of something.

Too Hard or Too Dry

Is your treat crunchy, but not in a good way? Is it an instant pile of crumbs? Here are some possibilities:

1. **They baked too long.** Overbaked treats can dry out and sometimes even burn.

2. **The oven bakes too hot.** You may have the oven set at 350°F, but your oven may just run hot. You can get a special oven thermometer at almost any store that sells cooking supplies. Place it inside your oven. If it reads less or more than what you set the oven at, you may need to adjust your temperature when you cook.

3. **There is too much of the dry ingredients in the batter.** You may be able to use the rest of your batter by carefully adding a tablespoon of water or milk at a time. Only add a little at a time so your batter doesn't become too runny.

4. **The batter was overmixed.** Whipping a batter too much (especially with a powerful mixer!) can cause your treats to get hard and crumbly sometimes. Pay attention to the recipe—if it says "mix until combined," you don't need to let the mixer run for 5 minutes after that point.

Too Much Spread

OK, they looked fine going into the oven, but they came out as giant puddles that mushed into each other instead of nice-size treats. What happened here?

1. **There was too much of the wet ingredients.** Was there a little too much liquid? Were the eggs maybe on the large side? You can try to add flour a teaspoon at a time to a dough that is too drippy.

2. **The butter was too warm.** Did the dough chill if the recipe asked for it? Did the butter melt when it should have been at room temperature? You may be able to save the rest of the batch by chilling your dough. If you're pinched for time, try grating the butter before adding it so it softens faster—but don't let it get too warm!

Unwanted Crunchy Bits

Did eggshell get in the batter? Finding a bit of hard eggshell is no fun. Crack the eggs carefully. One way to separate eggs is to use the big eggshell pieces to separate egg whites from yolks. Another way to separate eggs is to place your hands over a bowl and crack the egg into your hand, then carefully hold the yolk while the whites drip down into the bowl.

Frosting Texture Problems

When frosting or glaze is too thin or drippy, try beating in more powdered sugar ¼ cup at a time until it's a spreadable texture. If the frosting is too thick, try beating milk into your frosting 1 tablespoon at a time until it's right.

HOLIDAY GIFTING

Wait, before you take that treat with you, take a few seconds to make sure you're traveling in style! Here are a few tips on packing up and presenting your treats—plus ways to make sure they don't suffer from any holiday travels.

Customize. Write your friend's name in icing or add sprinkles in your mom's favorite color. The best extra touches come from the heart.

Change up the wrappers. Most holidays have fun cupcake liners available. Solid-colored cupcake liners or even shiny silver or gold liners look great, too! For a cozy look, use parchment paper liners.

Add some gift trimmings. For treats like cookies that don't smoosh, you can add plastic wrap and a bow. Also add a tag with their name!

Think about the container. Food containers from the grocery store can sometimes be reused to transport your treats. Peel off labels, clean, and dry well before using. You can also find inexpensive holiday tins at the craft store.

Protect from squishing. Think about how your packaging will protect your treat. Will it keep it from crumbling, breaking, or being squashed?

Bring a platter. If you're headed to a party, you can bring a separate serving platter and rearrange your treat when you arrive!

Grab a few forks. Don't forget serving utensils! Will napkins, plates, and forks be available? If not, make sure to supply what you'll need—like a cake server or toothpicks.

ABOUT THE RECIPES

There are many delicious recipes in this book, and I can't wait for you to make them. This book is divided by season, and you'll find all kinds of different holiday ideas between the pages. From chocolatey (try the Chocolate-Peppermint Crinkle Cookies on page 125) to fruity (the Raspberry Sweetheart Rolls on page 137 have only a few ingredients) and from silly (fake out your family with the April Fools' Tostada Cookies on page 33) to pretty (the Mermaid Brownie Pops on page 61), there is a recipe for everyone! (Oh, and if you need the perfect cake? Check out the Choco-Vanilla Birthday Cake on page 143 that works for almost any holiday.)

Tips to Help Along the Way

In this book there are four different types of tips to help you as you bake:

Try Instead: Look for this for a cool way to change the recipe a little.

Did You Know? Find fun info about ingredients or holidays here!

Helpful Hint: These let you know how to get your technique just right.

Troubleshooting: These can help prevent and fix common mistakes.

Everyone Makes Messes (and Mistakes)

Take a deep breath and remember this: Whenever you try something new, you are likely to make a few mistakes and maybe even a few messes along the way. It will be OK!

- Remember baking is fun! Use YOUR creativity.

- Make these recipes yours. Try new ideas as you learn more about baking.

- Hold your chin up high when something doesn't go as planned. You are an awesome baker, so keep going.

- Sometimes, it just won't look pretty, but it'll still taste great. Once, on a gingerbread house that just didn't work out, I grabbed a plastic toy dinosaur, washed it, and pretended like he'd stomped the house in a rampage! It was a crowd-pleaser.

Seriously, remember it's OK if your treats aren't perfect. The more you bake, the better you will get!

SUBSTITUTIONS & ALLERGENS

While most people love a sweet treat, you may have friends or family who can't have certain foods. Sometimes they can't join in on dessert, or they might ask everyone to bring a dish without a specific ingredient, like nuts or gluten. While every person is different in what they can and can't eat, here are a few ideas to adapt some of your own baked goods so even more friends and family can enjoy them.

When you make a substitution in a batter or recipe, remember texture, taste, and appearance may change. Watch your cook times carefully. Not every substitute will work perfectly every time—but it's worth it to make sure everyone can enjoy your treats.

- Gluten is found in flour and certain grains, but there are lots of products now on shelves that can accommodate folks who need to stay gluten-free. There are several brands of great gluten-free flour blends. Recipes with graham cracker crusts can substitute a gluten-free alternative. Also try my super-fudgy Gooey Passover Double-Chocolate Flourless Cookies on page 36—they are already gluten-free!

- When someone is dairy-free, it means they don't consume milk, cream, or cheese. Someone who has a vegan or plant-based diet also does not eat eggs. Almond milk, coconut milk, and other milk alternatives can sometimes be substituted in baking. A common egg-free substitute in baking is to make an egg substitute from flaxseed. Mix 1 tablespoon of ground flaxseed in 3 tablespoons of water and let it sit for 10 minutes, then use it in your recipe in place of eggs. You can also use ¼ cup of fruit puree in place of 1 egg in many recipes—so sometimes the answer can be using unsweetened applesauce or pumpkin puree.

- Nut allergies are very common. In this book, at the top of every recipe, you'll see a nut-free label if the recipe doesn't contain nuts or if nuts are optional.

Lemonade Bunny
Thumbprint Cookies,
page 28

2

spring

Spring is all about blooming flowers, fresh starts, and new beginnings! In this chapter, you'll find fresh fruity ideas with bunnies, flowers, and spring chicks! During this time of year, families are celebrating Easter, Passover, Mother's Day, Cinco de Mayo, and Eid al-Fitr. If you like being sneaky, try the April Fools' Tostada Cookies on page 33.

Lemonade Bunny Thumbprint Cookies

PREP TIME: 30 minutes | **BAKE TIME:** 23 to 24 minutes | **YIELD:** 20 cookies

Legend has it that the Easter Bunny lays, decorates, and hides colorful eggs every year as a symbol of new life. These bunnies are hiding a sweet lemonade cookie, perfect for a treat! Fresh and sweet, these cookies feel like spring sunshine. Decorate these funny bunnies fast, as they stay warm for only a little while before they set!

TOOLS/EQUIPMENT

- Baking sheet
- Parchment paper
- Zester or box grater with a fine grate
- Electric mixer or stand mixer

1 lemon
½ cup (1 stick) unsalted butter, at room temperature
¼ cup, plus 2 tablespoons powdered sugar
1¼ cups all-purpose flour
½ teaspoon salt
20 whole white candy melts, plus 20 white candy melts cut in half
40 candy eyes
Flat round sprinkles

PREHEAT THE OVEN TO 325°F.

Line the baking sheet with parchment paper.

ZEST AND JUICE THE LEMONS.

Rinse the lemon well and dry it. Use a metal zester or the smallest holes on a box grater to gently zest the outside of the lemon until you have about 1 teaspoon of yellow zest. Be careful to zest the yellow part of the lemon and not much of the white part underneath. Cut the same lemon in half and use your hands to squeeze the juice into a small bowl.

MIX THE WET INGREDIENTS.

In a large mixing bowl with an electric mixer, or in the bowl of a stand mixer, combine the butter, 2 tablespoons of powdered sugar, the lemon zest, and lemon juice.

MIX THE DRY INGREDIENTS AND COMBINE.

In a medium bowl, combine the flour, the remaining ¼ cup of powdered sugar, and the salt, mixing well with a big spoon. Add the flour mixture to the liquid mixture and mix. At first your dough will look sandy, but then it will start to form into a big ball. If it continues to look sandy, it's too dry—you can add ½ teaspoon of water.

Trouble-shooting:

Zest only the yellow thin outer skin of the lemon. If you zest too far, you begin to zest the white layer called the pith. This can give your cookies more of a bitter taste. Scrape against the shredder only two or three times before turning the lemon.

ROLL AND CHILL THE COOKIE DOUGH.

Roll the dough into small 1-inch balls, slightly smaller than a ping-pong ball. Place the balls on a baking sheet with about 1 inch between each. Freeze the dough on the baking sheet in the freezer for 15 minutes.

BAKE THE COOKIES.

Bake your cookies for 10 minutes. Remove from the oven and use the bottom of a ½ teaspoon measure to press a dent in the top of each cookie. Place the cookies back in the oven for 13 to 14 minutes. Check with a spatula that they have browned just a little on the bottom.

DECORATE AND TURN THE COOKIES INTO BUNNIES.

While the cookies are still warm, work quickly and place a round white candy melt in the center of each cookie. Place 2 cut candy melts at the top of each cookie for ears, making sure the candies touch in the center. Decorate with candy eyes and sprinkles for noses.

Easter Chick Surprise! Cupcakes

PREP TIME: 30 minutes | **BAKE TIME:** 16 to 18 minutes | **YIELD:** 14 to 16 cupcakes

Squawk! It's spring, and these cupcakes are laying eggs! Both Easter chicks and Easter eggs represent joy and new life. Your family and friends will grin when they discover the secret egg surprise inside these cupcakes. The idea of giving chocolate eggs for Easter goes back to Germany almost 200 years ago. Now kids all over the world celebrate with chocolate eggs.

TOOLS/EQUIPMENT

- Muffin pan
- Cupcake liners
- Electric mixer or stand mixer
- Toothpick
- Wire cooling rack or kitchen towel

FOR THE CUPCAKES

¾ cup granulated sugar
2 large eggs
1 tablespoon vanilla extract
½ cup oil
½ cup yogurt
1¼ cups all-purpose flour
1¼ teaspoons baking powder
½ teaspoon baking soda
½ teaspoon salt
1 cup mini colored chocolate eggs or mini colored chocolate candies

PREHEAT THE OVEN TO 350°F.

Line the muffin pan with cupcake liners.

MIX THE CUPCAKE BATTER.

In a large mixing bowl with an electric mixer or in the bowl of a stand mixer, add the granulated sugar, eggs, 1 tablespoon of vanilla, the oil, and yogurt. Mix for a minute or so until combined. In a medium bowl, combine the flour, baking powder, baking soda, and salt. Add the dry ingredients to the wet ingredients in the larger bowl and mix gently together. Your batter should now look like a thin pudding. Fill the cupcake liners about two-thirds full with batter.

BAKE THE CUPCAKES.

Bake the cupcakes for 16 to 18 minutes. Cupcakes are done when a toothpick inserted into the center comes out clean. Let the cupcakes cool completely on a wire rack as soon as they are cool enough to pull from the muffin pan.

FOR THE BUTTERCREAM FROSTING

½ cup (1 stick) unsalted butter, at room temperature
2 cups powdered sugar
1 teaspoon vanilla extract
2 tablespoons milk

FOR THE DECORATIONS

4 ounces yellow sprinkles
6 orange gummy candies
30 candy eyes

MAKE THE BUTTERCREAM FROSTING.

In a clean large mixing bowl or the bowl of a stand mixer, add the butter and beat on medium for 5 minutes. The butter will turn a paler color. Scrape the sides of the bowl with a spatula. Add the powdered sugar slowly, ½ cup at a time. Mix the frosting first on low, then medium, until all the sugar is mixed into the butter. Add 1 teaspoon of vanilla and the milk, then beat for 1 to 2 minutes more on medium speed.

ADD THE FILLING TO THE CUPCAKES.

With a sharp knife, cut a hole in the top of the cupcake and gently remove the top. You can also use a large icing tip to cut the hole by pushing it gently into the cupcake (try the tip labeled 1M, if you have one). Place the chocolate eggs inside the cupcake, then gently put the top back on the cupcake.

FROST THE CUPCAKES.

With a butter knife or icing spatula, frost the top of the cupcakes, covering the circle hiding the chocolates. Add some of your sprinkles to a small bowl. Work in small batches, frosting and then gently dipping the frosted cupcakes one at a time in the sprinkles.

DECORATE THE CUPCAKES.

Cut your gummy candy into small triangle pieces. Add candy eyes. Add orange gummy triangles as beaks.

Did You Know? One type of chicken called the Easter Egger does lay real colored eggs that can be blue, green, and even pink!

April Fools'
Tostada Cookies,
page 33

April Fools' Tostada Cookies

PREP TIME: 25 minutes | **BAKE TIME:** 14 to 16 minutes | **YIELD:** 6 to 7 giant cookies

April Fools! These may look like zesty and delicious open-faced tacos…but when your family takes a bite, SURPRISE! It's a giant coconut frosted cookie, sweet and tasty all the way through! The origin of April Fools' Day is surrounded in mystery—no one really knows how it got started. One idea is that April Fools' Day is tied to the first day of spring for the northern hemisphere—right around when Mother Nature was always fooling people with unpredictable weather.

TOOLS/EQUIPMENT

- 2 baking sheets
- Parchment paper
- Electric mixer or stand mixer (optional)
- Rolling pin
- 2 chopsticks (optional)
- 4½-inch bowl or plate
- 2 sandwich bags

FOR THE COOKIES

1 cup (2 sticks) unsalted butter, cold
1 cup granulated sugar
½ teaspoon vanilla extract
2 large eggs, cold
3¼ cups all-purpose flour, plus extra for rolling
½ teaspoon salt

PREHEAT THE OVEN TO 350°F.
Line the baking sheets with parchment paper.

MIX THE COOKIE DOUGH.
Slice each cold butter stick into 10 to 12 pieces and let sit on the counter for 5 minutes. In the bowl of your stand mixer or in a large mixing bowl with a strong wooden spoon, cream 1 cup of cold butter with the granulated sugar until well mixed. Add ½ teaspoon of vanilla and eggs, then mix the dough on low for 1 to 2 minutes until you see no more big chunks of butter. Add the flour and salt, then mix until a dough forms. You should be able to squeeze it together like Play-Doh.

ROLL OUT THE COOKIE DOUGH.
Lightly flour a clean counter and the rolling pin. Roll out your dough, adding flour to the top of your dough. Lay two chopsticks on either side of your dough. Roll until it is about ⅜ inch thick, a little thicker than a chopstick.

› CONTINUED

FOR THE FROSTING AND TOPPINGS

1 cup shredded sweetened coconut

Green and yellow food coloring

½ cup (1 stick) unsalted butter, at room temperature

2 cups powdered sugar, plus 1 tablespoon

1 teaspoon vanilla extract

3 tablespoons milk, divided

1 tablespoon unsweetened cocoa powder

7 red gummy bears or red gummy candies (optional)

CUT AND BAKE THE COOKIES.

Using the 4½-inch bowl, cut out giant cookies by tracing the bowl with a butter knife. Place the cookies on the baking sheets and bake for 14 to 16 minutes, until the cookies feel like they have a skin across the top but are still pale. The cookies will continue to bake and harden a little on the baking sheet as they cool for a few minutes.

MAKE THE "CHEESE" AND "LETTUCE."

Place ½ cup of coconut in each plastic sandwich bag. Add 3 drops of green food coloring and 2 drops of yellow food coloring for "lettuce" to one bag. In the second bag of coconut, add 4 drops of yellow food coloring for "cheese." Close both bags and shake to mix the colors. Once mixed, open the bags and spread the contents of each each on a plate to let the coconut dry for a few minutes.

MAKE THE BUTTERCREAM FROSTING.

In a large bowl with an electric mixer or in the bowl of a stand mixer, beat ½ cup of room-temperature butter on medium-high speed for 5 minutes. Your butter will turn a paler color. Scrape the sides of the bowl with a spatula, then slowly add 2 cups of powdered sugar a little at a time. Mix on low speed, then medium, until all the sugar is well mixed into the butter. Add 1 teaspoon of vanilla and 2 tablespoons of milk and beat for 1 to 2 minutes more on medium speed.

COLOR THE BUTTERCREAM TO MAKE BEANS AND
SOUR CREAM.

Remove ½ cup of buttercream from the bowl. In a
small bowl combine the cocoa, the remaining 1 tablespoon of milk, and 1 tablespoon of powdered sugar
and mix. Use this mixture to make brown buttercream
the color of refried beans. The extra white buttercream is now the "sour cream."

DECORATE THE TOSTADA COOKIES.

Spread a layer of brown "bean" frosting across all
cookies evenly. Sprinkle both colors of coconut
across the cookies. Add a small dollop of white
buttercream "sour cream" to the center of each
cookie. You can also slice red gummies to make diced
"tomatoes."

Try Instead: You can make these
cookies in a smaller size, but they will bake
much faster. Start checking them after
8 to 9 minutes of bake time and check often.

Gooey Passover Double-Chocolate Flourless Cookies

PREP TIME: 15 minutes | **BAKE TIME:** 13 to 14 minutes | **YIELD:** 18 cookies

Who can say no to an ooey-gooey double-chocolate cookie? Passover is the perfect time to make these delicious chocolatey treats. The holiday is celebrated over 8 days by the Jewish community and is full of family time and other special foods. Bring these chocolatey cookies, and the whole family will want to celebrate together!

TOOLS/EQUIPMENT
- 2 baking sheets
- Parchment paper
- Electric mixer or stand mixer

---

3 cups powdered sugar

7 tablespoons unsweetened cocoa powder

¼ teaspoon salt

3 egg whites

1 teaspoon vanilla extract

1 cup semisweet chocolate chips

1 cup chopped walnuts or pecans (optional)

PREHEAT THE OVEN TO 350°F.
Line the baking sheets with parchment paper.

MIX YOUR DRY INGREDIENTS INTO A BATTER.
In a large bowl with an electric mixer or in the bowl of a stand mixer, slowly mix together the powdered sugar, cocoa powder, and salt until combined.

CRACK AND SEPARATE YOUR EGGS.
Crack the eggs and carefully separate the egg yolks from the egg whites. Do this over a bowl by catching the egg yolk in one half of your eggshell while letting the egg white drain into the bowl. You can also do the same thing with the palms of your hands if you find it easier (the liquid whites will leak out through your fingers). Focus on not breaking the egg yolk and keeping eggshell out of your cookie batter. Hold on to the egg whites and discard or save the yolks. (You can use one yolk in a batch of "You're a Smart Cookie" Graduation Cookies on page 52).

MIX THE COOKIE DOUGH BATTER.
Add the egg whites and vanilla to the dry ingredients. Mix on low and then bump up to medium until a batter forms. The batter should be thick and slightly runny. Sometimes your batter may be too thick, depending on the size of your eggs. If the batter looks more like the

texture of chocolate frosting, add 1 tablespoon of water and whip again. Fold in the semisweet chocolate chips and pecans or walnuts (if using).

SCOOP THE BATTER ONTO THE PARCHMENT PAPER.
Use a tablespoon measure and scoop the batter onto the baking sheets. Leave room (at least 3 inches or so) between cookies. Scoop 6 cookies per pan—the cookies will spread and puff up a lot while baking!

BAKE THE COOKIES UNTIL THEY ARE FUDGY!
Bake the cookies for 13 to 14 minutes. The inside will be slightly gooey (including the chocolate chips!) but not spilling out of the cookies. Let the cookies completely cool on the parchment paper. Once cool, gently peel the cookies from the parchment paper with your hands. These cookies are fragile, and a spatula can break them as they continue to set. Enjoy your fudgy cookies!

Raspberry and Cream
Cheese Cupcakes,
page 39

Raspberry and Cream Cheese Cupcakes

PREP TIME: 30 minutes | **BAKE TIME:** 17 to 18 minutes | **YIELD:** 14 to 16 cupcakes

Mom will be so surprised when you make her these Raspberry and Cream Cheese Cupcakes for Mother's Day! Did you know that pink and light red flowers stand for gratitude and appreciation? That matches perfectly with these delicious cupcakes. Add mini chocolate chips, chocolate shreds, or sprinkles for a finishing touch.

TOOLS/EQUIPMENT

- Muffin pan
- Cupcake liners
- Electric mixer or stand mixer
- Toothpick
- Wire cooling rack
- Piping bag or strong plastic zip-top bag

FOR THE CUPCAKES

6 ounces fresh raspberries (1 small clamshell), divided

1¼ cups all-purpose flour, plus 2 teaspoons

1¼ teaspoons baking powder

½ teaspoon baking soda

½ teaspoon salt

2 large eggs

¾ cup granulated sugar

½ cup oil

½ cup yogurt

2 teaspoons vanilla extract

PREHEAT THE OVEN TO 350°F.

Line the muffin pan with cupcake liners.

WASH AND DICE THE RASPBERRIES.

Wash and dry the raspberries. Remove 14 of your raspberries (about ½ cup) for decorating the cupcakes and set aside. Cut the remaining raspberries (about 4 ounces or 1 cup) into small pieces. Put the raspberries in a small bowl and add 2 teaspoons of flour. Stir the raspberries and flour, then set aside.

MIX THE CUPCAKE BATTER.

In a large mixing bowl, add 1¼ cups of flour, the baking powder, baking soda, and salt. Mix. In a separate medium mixing bowl with an electric mixer or in the bowl of a stand mixer, beat the eggs. Add the granulated sugar, oil, yogurt, and 2 teaspoons of vanilla to the eggs, mixing on medium or until combined. Fold the floured raspberry pieces into your batter.

BAKE THE CUPCAKES.

Fill each cupcake liner about three-quarters full with batter. Bake for 17 to 18 minutes, or until a toothpick comes out clean when inserted into a cupcake. Allow the cupcakes to cool completely on a wire cooling rack.

› CONTINUED

FOR THE FROSTING

1 cup (2 sticks) unsalted butter, at room temperature
8 ounces cream cheese, at room temperature
4 cups powdered sugar
2 teaspoons vanilla extract
Sprinkles or small chocolate pieces, for decorating (optional)

MAKE THE CREAM CHEESE FROSTING.
Cream the butter on medium speed for 4 to 5 minutes with a stand mixer or electric mixer, scraping down the sides of the bowl with a silicone spatula. Cut the cream cheese into chunks and cream with the butter for 2 to 3 minutes on medium speed until smooth. Scrape down the sides of the bowl with a spatula. Add the powdered sugar 1 cup at a time, mixing first on low speed, then on medium until well mixed, scraping down the sides of the bowl each time before you add more sugar. Once mixed, add 2 teaspoons of vanilla and mix for 1 minute more.

FROST AND DECORATE THE CUPCAKES.
Fill a piping bag or zip-top bag with frosting using the guidance on page 19. In the center of the cupcake, build a little mound of frosting about 1 inch high, working in circles. Now move to the outer edge of the cupcake in circles. Slowly swirl up the inside frosting to make a nice twisted frosting that looks like the top of an ice cream cone. Top each cupcake with a fresh raspberry. You can also add mini chocolate chips, sprinkles, or grated chocolate shreds to decorate.

Try Instead: Strawberries also work well in this recipe. You'll need 1 cup of diced strawberries for the inside of the cupcakes and extra for decorating! Prepare as described above.

Sweet Orange Hamantaschen (Hat) Cookies

PREP TIME: 30 minutes | **BAKE TIME:** 12 to 14 minutes | **YIELD:** 16 to 18 cookies

Hamantaschen are yummy cookies often made for the Jewish holiday of Purim. Filled with a gooey filling, a circle of dough is folded to look like a three-corner hat similar to what Haman (one of the characters in the holiday's story) wore. While hamantaschen are traditionally filled with jam, they are sometimes also filled with nuts, poppy seeds, or even chocolate hazelnut spread.

TOOLS/EQUIPMENT

- 2 baking sheets
- Parchment paper
- Rolling pin
- 3½-inch circle cookie cutter or drinking glass
- Whisk (optional)
- Silicone brush

4 large eggs, divided
1 tablespoon orange zest
¼ cup orange juice
1 teaspoon vanilla extract
1 cup sugar
½ cup oil
4 cups all-purpose flour, plus extra for dusting the work surface
2 teaspoons baking powder
¼ teaspoon salt
1 tablespoon water
½ cup jam (apricot, raspberry, strawberry, you choose!)

PREHEAT THE OVEN TO 400°F.

Line the baking sheets with parchment paper.

MIX THE DOUGH.

In a medium mixing bowl, crack 2 eggs and beat. Add the orange zest, orange juice, vanilla, sugar, and oil. Whisk well until combined. In a large bowl, combine 4 cups of flour, the baking powder, and salt. Add the wet ingredients to the dry ingredients and mix them together well.

KNEAD THE DOUGH WITH YOUR HANDS.

Once the dough starts coming together into a ball, knead the dough with your hands for 1 or 2 minutes, until it's a pretty solid dough ball. Then place the dough ball on your lightly floured work surface.

ROLL OUT THE DOUGH AND CUT OUT YOUR COOKIES.

Roll the dough to about ¼ inch thick with a rolling pin. With a round cookie cutter or a glass that is 3½ inches across, cut out your cookies.

MAKE AN EGG WASH FOR THE COOKIES.

Crack the last 2 eggs into a bowl with the water. Beat with a whisk or fork to make an egg wash.

› CONTINUED

FOLD, PRESS, AND FILL THE COOKIES.

In the center of each cookie, place 1 teaspoon of jam. Using extra jam at this step will cause the cookies to overflow, so only use 1 teaspoon! With a silicone brush or your fingers, swipe a thin layer of egg on the outer edge of the circle. Fold the circles into a triangle by folding pieces from the outer circle in like a triangle-shaped hat, pressing the corners down together gently as you fold. Fold halfway to the center, leaving jam in the center of the cookie. Use your brush to cover the entire top of the cookie with a coat of egg wash.

BAKE THE COOKIES.

Place the cookies on the baking sheets. Bake for 12 to 14 minutes. Remove the cookies carefully from the oven, then let them cool. These cookies will be cakey and just a little crumbly.

Helpful Hint: Some people try to pinch the corners shut on these cookies, but they often will loosen as they cook. Pressing down on the corners toward the table and being generous with the egg wash help the cookies stay together.

Ultimate Fiesta Chocolate Churro Cups

PREP TIME: 20 minutes | **BAKE TIME:** 12 to 14 minutes | **YIELD:** 9 churro cups

These churro cups turn churros inside out! Churros are served with chocolate or caramel sauce and are a yummy treat for Cinco de Mayo. Use a good chocolate for the ganache sauce—it makes a big difference in the taste. If you are eating these later, wait until right before you serve them to add the chocolate sauce.

TOOLS/EQUIPMENT

- Muffin pan
- Cutting board
- Silicone brush
- Microwave
- Whisk

Cooking oil spray, for greasing the pan

All-purpose flour, for the work surface

1 sheet frozen puff pastry dough, thawed according to package instructions

¼ cup sugar

1 tablespoon cinnamon

2 tablespoons unsalted butter, melted

⅔ cup chocolate chips or chopped chocolate

½ cup heavy (whipping) cream

PREHEAT THE OVEN TO 350°F.

Prep the muffin pan by spraying with cooking oil spray.

PREP THE PUFF PASTRY DOUGH.

Lightly flour your cutting board with flour. When the defrosted puff pastry is soft, unroll it and lay it flat. Using a sharp knife, cut the dough into 9 equal pieces like a tic-tac-toe board. Use a fork to prick small holes in each square four to six times.

BAKE THE DOUGH.

Place each square of dough in a muffin cup and push down. Bake for 12 to 14 minutes, until they are a golden-brown color. Let them cool in the pan.

MIX YOUR CINNAMON SUGAR.

In a medium bowl, mix together the sugar and cinnamon.

BRUSH WITH BUTTER AND SPRINKLE CINNAMON SUGAR ON THE CHURROS.

Brush the melted butter onto the churro cups in the pan with a silicone brush, then move the churro cups to a big plate. With a spoon, sprinkle cinnamon sugar all over the cups and tap off any loose cinnamon sugar.

› CONTINUED

MAKE CHOCOLATE GANACHE SAUCE AND DRIZZLE ON
THE CHURROS.

Put the chocolate chips (or chopped chocolate) in a medium glass bowl. In another medium glass bowl, heat the heavy cream in the microwave until it just begins to boil, about 1 minute. Pour the cream over the chocolate and whisk until the chocolate is smooth, 2 to 3 minutes. Add a spoonful of chocolate to each churro cup and serve immediately!

Helpful Hint: When the churro cups come out of the oven, they are super puffy. Use a spoon to push the middle down again if you need to make room for the chocolate sauce.

Troubleshooting: If your chocolate doesn't dissolve all the way when adding the cream, melt it more in the microwave on low in 20-second bursts, stirring in between, until melted.

Ultimate Fiesta
Chocolate Churro Cups,
page 43

Blooming Brownies

PREP TIME: 30 minutes | **BAKE TIME:** 30 to 35 minutes | **YIELD:** 8 to 10 brownies

The flowers are blooming, the grass is sprouting, and so are these brownies! Whether you are ringing in spring with Easter or May Day or just celebrating the new green buds in your garden, these flowery brownies need to be on your list to make! Fill this brownie garden with marshmallow flowers, or even sneak a few bunnies and jelly beans into the spring party.

TOOLS/EQUIPMENT

- 8- or 9-inch square baking pan
- Parchment paper
- Pencil (optional)
- Clean kitchen scissors (optional)
- Whisk
- Electric mixer or stand mixer
- Microwave
- Zip-top bags

FOR THE BROWNIES

Oil, for greasing pan
3 large eggs
½ cup (1 stick) unsalted butter, melted
½ cup brown sugar
½ cup granulated sugar
2 teaspoons vanilla extract
½ cup all-purpose flour
½ cup unsweetened cocoa powder
¼ teaspoon salt
1 cup chocolate chips

PREHEAT YOUR OVEN TO 350°F.
Line your baking pan with parchment paper and oil the sides of the pan well. You can cut the parchment paper to be the same size as your pan by tracing the bottom with a pencil and then cutting the paper with scissors.

MIX THE BROWNIE BATTER.
Whisk the eggs together briskly until well blended and bubbly in a large mixing bowl. Add ½ cup of melted butter, the brown sugar, granulated sugar, and 2 teaspoons of vanilla to the eggs, whisking until well combined. In a medium mixing bowl, combine the flour, cocoa powder, and salt and mix well. Next, add the dry mixture to the wet ingredients and blend together with a whisk. Lastly, fold in 1 cup of chocolate chips.

BAKE THE BROWNIES.
Fill your pan with brownie batter and bake at 350°F for 30 to 35 minutes. The batter will still be a little gooey inside, but not raw. Chill the brownies in a refrigerator or freezer until cool, at least 15 to 20 minutes.

FOR THE FROSTING

½ cup (1 stick) unsalted butter, at room temperature
2 cups powdered sugar
1 teaspoon vanilla extract
2 tablespoons milk
½ cup semisweet chocolate chips

FOR THE DECORATIONS

6 to 8 chocolate sandwich cookies
Colored sugar sprinkles
6 to 10 large marshmallows
6 to 8 chocolate candies
Green sprinkles
Easter marshmallow bunnies or chicks (optional)
Jelly beans (optional)

 Try Instead: Instead of sprinkles, use bright green coconut, like in the April Fools' Tostada Cookies on page 33.

MAKE THE CHOCOLATE FROSTING.

With an electric or stand mixer, beat the room-temperature butter on medium-high speed for 5 minutes. Scrape the bowl with a spatula, then add the powdered sugar ½ cup at a time. Mix until all the sugar is mixed into the butter. Add 1 teaspoon of vanilla and the milk and beat for 1 to 2 minutes more on medium speed. Put ½ cup of chocolate chips in a small glass bowl. Melt the chocolate chips in the microwave for 20 seconds on half power, then stir, repeating until melted. Stir with a dry spoon or the chocolate will seize (become thick and grainy). Add the melted chocolate to the frosting and mix. Remove 2 to 3 tablespoons of frosting and set aside in a separate bowl for decorating.

FROST THE BROWNIES AND SPRINKLE COOKIE "DIRT."

Remove the brownies from the pan once cool. Frost the brownies with the chocolate frosting in an even layer. Place chocolate sandwich cookies in a zip-top bag and gently crush. Sprinkle the cookie crumbs over the brownies.

DECORATE THE BROWNIES.

Place the colored sugar sprinkles in small bowls, one per color. Cut marshmallows at a diagonal to make 2 triangles. While the marshmallow is still sticky, dip the cut side of marshmallow in colored sugar. Use the extra frosting to attach the marshmallows, colored-side up. Four marshmallows plus a chocolate candy in the center make a flower. Sprinkle green sprinkles and decorate with any other Easter or spring candies.

Eid Moon Cookies,
page 49

Eid Moon Cookies

PREP TIME: 30 minutes | **BAKE TIME:** 12 to 14 minutes | **YIELD:** 24 to 26 small cookies

Eid means "feast" or "festival" and is celebrated every year at the end of Ramadan. The holiday is based on the lunar calendar and is a day for having celebrations with family and friends. These modern lunar cookies feature a marbleized royal icing that is made from meringue powder, giving them a galaxy look. Have a feast with your family and friends with these delicious cookies!

TOOLS/EQUIPMENT

- 2 baking sheets
- Parchment paper
- Stand mixer (optional)
- Rolling pin
- 2 chopsticks (optional)
- 3-inch circle cookie cutter or drinking glass
- Wire cooling rack or kitchen towel
- Toothpick (optional)

FOR THE COOKIES

½ cup (1 stick) unsalted butter, cold
½ cup granulated sugar
¼ teaspoon salt
¼ teaspoon vanilla extract
2 large eggs, cold
1½ cups all-purpose flour, plus more for rolling

PREHEAT THE OVEN TO 350°F.

Line the baking sheets with parchment paper.

MIX THE COOKIE DOUGH.

Slice your butter stick into 10 to 12 pieces. The butter should sit on the counter from the refrigerator for about 5 minutes, which keeps it a little colder than room-temperature butter. In a large bowl with a strong wooden spoon, or in the bowl of a stand mixer, cream together the butter, granulated sugar, and salt. Add ¼ teaspoon of vanilla and the eggs, then mix on low speed for 1 to 2 minutes, until you see no more big chunks of butter. If you are mixing by hand, this takes 4 to 5 minutes, and I recommend using a thick-handled wooden spoon, as the dough is thick. Add 1½ cups of flour and again mix on low speed until just combined, cutting the butter mixture into your flour. You should be able to squeeze the dough like Play-Doh.

> CONTINUED

FOR THE ICING

1 cup powdered sugar
1 tablespoon
    meringue powder
½ teaspoon
    vanilla extract
2 tablespoons water
Food coloring

ROLL OUT AND CUT OUT YOUR MOON COOKIES.

Lightly flour a clean counter and the rolling pin. Roll out your dough, adding flour to the top of your dough. Lay two chopsticks on either side of your dough. Roll until it is about ⅜ inch thick, a little thicker than a chopstick. Using your cookie cutter or drinking glass, cut a circle from your dough. Remove the circle from the dough, then line up your cookie cutter again over the dough—this time about halfway over your cookie—and cut to create a moon-shaped cookie to put on your pan. Add the remaining piece of dough inside the cutter to a scrap pile and repeat. When you can't cut any more cookies, reroll your dough with the scraps and repeat. Continue until you have cut all of your cookies.

BAKE THE COOKIES.

Bake the cookies for 12 to 14 minutes or until cooked through. Cookies will be slightly light brown on the bottom and light on top. They feel like they have a skin on top when done. Cool them on a wire rack or towel so they don't keep cooking on the hot pan.

MIX THE ICING.

This frosting is a royal icing that uses meringue powder, which can be found in many cake supply and craft stores. In a small bowl, combine the powdered sugar, meringue powder, ½ teaspoon of vanilla, and the water. Mix with a spoon until completely combined. If you don't have meringue powder, frost with my buttercream icing from the "You're a Smart Cookie" Graduation Cookies on page 52.

DIP THE COOKIES IN ICING.

Add 3 to 4 tablespoons of icing to a second bowl. Add a few drops of food coloring and mix well. (I like to use blue or purple for a galaxy look.) Carefully holding the cookie, dip it first into the white icing, and then gently into the colored icing, then set on a plate to dry. Your cookie will have a marbled look! You can also use spoons to drizzle icing or a toothpick to swirl it more if needed. To set the icing faster, place in the refrigerator for a few minutes.

Troubleshooting: Most sugar cookie dough requires you to chill the dough for a long time before rolling. Using cold ingredients and only a little mixing helps us avoid long chill times with this dough. If your dough does turn out too soft, you can pop it into the refrigerator or freezer for 30 minutes before rolling.

"You're a Smart Cookie" Graduation Cookies

PREP TIME: 45 minutes | **BAKE TIME:** 10 to 11 minutes | **YIELD:** 20 to 24 cookies

Graduation season is such an exciting time. All that hard schoolwork has paid off! Tell someone how proud you are of them with these "smart cookie" cookies! Use two colors of buttercream frosting to make glasses, eyes, and fun smiles! You can even make these cookies look like your friend or family member and decorate with icing in their school colors. These smart cookies are also a fun treat for back-to-school season.

TOOLS/EQUIPMENT

- 2 baking sheets
- Parchment paper
- Cookie scoop (optional)
- Electric mixer or stand mixer
- 2 piping bags or strong plastic zip-top bags

FOR THE COOKIE DOUGH

1 cup (2 sticks) unsalted butter, at room temperature
1 cup brown sugar
½ cup granulated sugar
1 large egg plus 1 egg yolk
1 teaspoon vanilla extract
2 cups all-purpose flour
1 teaspoon baking soda
½ teaspoon salt
1 cup chocolate chips
Candy eyes (optional)

FOR THE BUTTERCREAM FROSTING

½ cup (1 stick) unsalted butter, at room temperature
2 cups powdered sugar
1 teaspoon vanilla extract
2 tablespoons milk
Food coloring (optional)

PREHEAT THE OVEN TO 350°F.

Line the baking sheets with parchment paper.

MIX THE COOKIE DOUGH.

In a large mixing bowl, mix 1 cup of room-temperature butter, the brown sugar, granulated sugar, egg and egg yolk, and 1 teaspoon of vanilla until combined. In a medium bowl, mix the flour, baking soda, and salt until combined. Now combine the flour mixture with the sugar and butter mixture and mix well until combined. Then fold in the chocolate chips. Chill the dough for 15 minutes.

BAKE THE COOKIES.

Using a cookie scoop or tablespoon, scoop about 2 tablespoons of dough and roll into a ball. Place about 8 balls on each pan, leaving about 2 inches between each, and bake for 10 to 11 minutes, until crisp on the outside but still a bit gooey in the center.

MIX THE BUTTERCREAM FROSTING.

In a large bowl with an electric mixer or in the bowl of a stand mixer, whip ½ cup of room-temperature butter for 5 minutes on low speed and then medium. The butter will be lighter in color. Add the powdered sugar ½ cup at a time on low speed and then medium until combined. Add 1 teaspoon of vanilla and the milk and mix.

Helpful Hint: Hold the frosting bag in your writing hand, with your other hand holding the top of the bag so it stays twisted closed as you pipe.

COLOR THE BUTTERCREAM WITH FOOD COLORING.

If using food coloring, put half of the buttercream frosting in a small bowl. In each bowl of frosting slowly stir in food coloring, 2 to 3 drops at a time. Add the frosting into piping bags (or plastic zip-top bags). See the tips for filling a piping bag on page 19. Twist the top of the bag closed and snip a tiny hole at the tip for frosting to flow out of the bag.

DECORATE THE COOKIES WITH FROSTING FACES.

Attach the candy eyes with a tiny dollop of frosting. Use the frosting to draw faces on the cookies. I liked drawing glasses and smiles. You can draw eyelashes, winking eyes, smiles, and silly faces. Be creative!

Watermelon Pizza
Cookie Cake,
page 73

3

summer

Summer sunshine, swimming, backyard BBQs, and adventure is what this chapter is about! Celebrate holidays like Father's Day, Fourth of July, or Memorial Day with these yummy treats. Also find ideas for what to make when your baseball team wins, because you went berry picking, or to take on a camping trip. Don't miss the desserts perfect for after splashing around in a lake, pool, or ocean!

Ultimate Memorial Day Pound Cake

PREP TIME: 15 minutes | **BAKE TIME:** 65 to 75 minutes | **YIELD:** 12 slices

Memorial Day was originally called Decoration Day, because of the tradition of decorating with patriotic wreaths, flags, and flowers. The holiday is a day for honoring the military in the United States. Your family and friends will love this delicious pound cake decorated with red, white, and blue toppings. It's great for a party! Slices of pound cake also freeze well for later... if there's any left!

TOOLS/EQUIPMENT
- 9-inch loaf pan
- Plastic cling wrap
- Electric mixer or stand mixer (optional)
- Toothpick

½ cup (1 stick) unsalted butter, at room temperature, plus more for greasing the pan

1½ cups all-purpose flour, plus more for the pan

1 cup sugar

2 teaspoons vanilla extract

3 large eggs

½ teaspoon salt

½ teaspoon baking powder

½ cup sour cream

Whipped cream, for topping

Strawberries, blueberries, and raspberries, for decorating

PREHEAT YOUR OVEN TO 325°F.

BUTTER AND FLOUR THE LOAF PAN.
Grease all sides of the loaf pan inside well with butter, then add flour to your pan. Add plastic cling wrap to the top, tilt to coat all sides, then shake off any extra flour. You can also use a special baking spray with flour already in the oil. Discard the cling wrap.

MIX THE WET INGREDIENTS.
In a large bowl with a mixer or spoon, or in the bowl of a stand mixer, cream the butter with the sugar for 2 to 3 minutes, then add the vanilla and mix well. Add the eggs to the batter one at a time, mixing well in between each egg.

ADD THE DRY INGREDIENTS TO MAKE A CAKE BATTER.
In a medium mixing bowl, mix the flour, salt, and baking powder until well combined. Alternate adding half of the flour mixture, then ¼ cup of sour cream, then more flour and then the remaining ¼ cup of sour cream until everything is mixed. The batter will now be pale yellow and a little runny.

Try Instead: This cake is also delicious served with ice cream or topped with the glaze from the Raspberry Sweetheart Rolls on page 137.

BAKE THE CAKE.

Bake the cake for about 1 hour before you start checking if it is done. This is a dense but buttery cake—it takes a while to cook through to the center. It usually takes between 65 and 75 minutes in most ovens, until a toothpick inserted in the center comes out clean.

COOL, SLICE, AND DECORATE THE CAKE.

Remove the cake from the pan after it has cooled, then slice into thick slices. Decorate with whipped cream and fresh red and blue berries—such as strawberries, blueberries, and raspberries. (You can learn to make your own whipped cream on page 66.)

Red, White, and Blue
Emoji Cupcakes,
page 59

Red, White, and Blue Emoji Cupcakes

PREP TIME: 30 minutes | **BAKE TIME:** 15 to 16 minutes | **YIELD:** 12 to 14 cupcakes

Happy Fourth of July! These days we celebrate with fireworks and picnics, but did you know the Fourth of July wasn't recognized as a federal holiday until 1870? That's over 100 years after the USA was founded! Celebrate with these emoji cupcakes! Add smiles, heart eyes, sunglasses, and maybe even a few red, white, and blue flags.

TOOLS/EQUIPMENT

- Muffin pan
- Cupcake liners
- Electric mixer or stand mixer
- Whisk (optional)
- Toothpick
- Wire cooling rack or kitchen towel
- 2 piping bags or strong plastic zip-top bags

FOR THE CUPCAKES

½ cup (1 stick) unsalted butter, at room temperature

¾ cup granulated sugar

2 large eggs

½ cup yogurt

1 tablespoon vanilla extract

1⅓ cups all-purpose flour

1¼ teaspoons baking powder

½ teaspoon salt

⅓ cup red, white, and blue sprinkles (about 3 ounces)

PREHEAT THE OVEN TO 350°F.
Line the muffin pan with cupcake liners.

MIX THE WET INGREDIENTS.
In a medium bowl with an electric mixer or in the bowl of a stand mixer, cream together ½ cup of butter and the granulated sugar until soft and smooth. Beat the eggs in a small bowl with a whisk or fork, then mix them into the butter mixture. Add the yogurt and 1 tablespoon of vanilla and mix until combined.

MIX IN THE DRY INGREDIENTS TO MAKE A BATTER.
In a second medium bowl, combine the flour, baking powder, and salt until combined, then add to the wet ingredients and mix well. Fold the sprinkles into your batter.

BAKE THE CUPCAKES.
Fill each cupcake liner about two-thirds full with batter. Wipe any dribbles with a towel before the pan goes in the oven. Bake the cupcakes for 15 to 16 minutes, or until a toothpick inserted in the center comes out clean, then allow the cupcakes to cool on a towel or rack.

› CONTINUED

**FOR THE FROSTING
AND DECORATIONS**

1 cup (2 sticks) unsalted
    butter, at room
    temperature
4 cups powdered sugar
2 teaspoons
    vanilla extract
4 tablespoons milk
Red and blue food
    coloring
Red, white and blue
    sprinkles (optional)
Candy eyes (optional)

WHIP THE BUTTERCREAM FROSTING.
In a large bowl with an electric mixer or in the bowl of a
stand mixer, beat 1 cup of butter on medium-high speed
for 5 minutes. The butter will turn a paler color. Scrape
the sides of the bowl with a spatula then add the powdered sugar slowly, about ½ cup at a time, mixing slowly
at first and then faster. Add 2 teaspoons of vanilla and
the milk and mix until fluffy.

FROST THE CUPCAKES WITH FROSTING.
Use half of the buttercream to frost each cupcake white.
Use a spatula or knife to make the frosting smooth.

DECORATE THE CUPCAKES WITH EMOJIS.
Split the remaining frosting into two bowls. Mix red food
coloring into one bowl and blue food coloring into the
other. Use the advice on page 19 to put each color of
frosting into a piping bag or strong zip-top bag. Use the
frosting to draw emoji faces on your cupcakes. Try heart
eyes, smiley faces, sunglasses, winking faces, or even an
American flag emoji. Use sprinkles and candy eyes to
add extra details to your emojis.

Helpful Hint: If the cupcakes will be outside in
the hot summer heat for a long time, consider
swapping out one-third of the butter in the frosting
recipe for shortening. While butter will taste a bit
better, shortening will hold up better to a super-hot
summer day.

Mermaid Brownie Pops

PREP TIME: 30 minutes | **BAKE TIME:** 13 to 15 minutes | **YIELD:** 12 brownies

Summer always makes me think of a beach party! Make these beachy Mermaid Brownie Pops for your next beach, pool, backyard, or birthday party. These brownie pops bake up fast but do continue cooking in the pan. For the ultimate fudgy brownie, take them out of the pan as soon as you can and let them cool on a towel. Have fun decorating with mermaid scales!

TOOLS/EQUIPMENT

- Muffin pan
- Whisk (optional)
- Wire cooling rack or kitchen towel
- Electric mixer or stand mixer
- Piping bag or strong plastic zip-top bag
- 2 glasses

FOR THE BROWNIE POPS

Cooking oil spray, for greasing the pan

3 large eggs

½ cup (1 stick) unsalted butter, melted

½ cup brown sugar

½ cup granulated sugar

1 teaspoon vanilla extract

½ cup all-purpose flour

½ cup unsweetened cocoa powder

¼ teaspoon salt

⅔ cup white chocolate chips

PREHEAT YOUR OVEN TO 350°F.
Spray the muffin pan well with cooking oil spray.

MIX THE BROWNIE BATTER.
In a large mixing bowl, crack and beat your eggs with a whisk or a fork. Add ½ cup of melted butter, the brown sugar, granulated sugar, and 1 teaspoon of vanilla and mix until well combined. In a medium mixing bowl, mix the flour, cocoa, and salt until combined. Add the dry ingredients to the wet ingredients and mix well. Fold in the white chocolate chips.

BAKE YOUR BROWNIES.
Split the batter evenly between 12 muffin cups, about 1½ to 2 tablespoons of batter per muffin cup. Bake the brownies for 13 to 15 minutes, until fudgy in the middle but not raw. Remove the brownies from the pan and cool them the rest of the way on a rack or towel.

WHIP THE BUTTERCREAM FROSTING.
In a large mixing bowl with an electric mixer or in the bowl of a stand mixer, beat ½ cup of room-temperature butter on medium-high speed for 5 minutes. Scrape down the sides of the bowl, then add the powdered sugar slowly, about ½ cup at a time, whipping well. Add 1 teaspoon of vanilla and the milk and beat for 1 to 2 minutes more on medium speed.

› CONTINUED

FOR THE BUTTERCREAM FROSTING

½ cup (1 stick) unsalted butter, at room temperature
2 cups powdered sugar
1 teaspoon vanilla extract
2 tablespoons milk

FOR THE DECORATIONS

Food coloring
12 wooden Popsicle sticks
Sprinkles

COLOR THE FROSTING FOR DECORATING.

Split the frosting between two small bowls. Color each bowl of frosting by mixing in food coloring a few drops at a time. I like purple and teal. Put each color of frosting into a piping bag or zip-top bag by following the instructions on page 19.

FROST AND DECORATE BROWNIES WITH MERMAID SCALES.

Put a Popsicle stick in each brownie. With the frosting, make a row of small button-sized circles across the top of a brownie. Using a butter knife, pull the frosting straight down just a little to create a fish scale. Add a second layer of button-sized frosting dots on the bottom of the first row. Again pull the bottom of the frosting down. Continue to the bottom of the brownie, then add sprinkles.

> **Helpful Hint:** Don't worry about making your frosting dots perfect, as you will be pulling them down with your butter knife anyway. Focus on layering the frosting dots so they look more like fish scales.

Camping Party S'mores Cookies

PREP TIME: 20 minutes | **BAKE TIME:** 10 to 12 minutes | **YIELD:** 12 cookies

Whether you love to sleep outside or prefer to just hang around a campfire, you'll love the gooey combo of graham crackers, chocolate, and marshmallow in these s'mores cookies. National S'mores Day is August 10, another reason to celebrate! These cookies are made with all brown sugar instead of granulated to give them an almost smoky flavor like a campfire. They're also portable enough for a picnic!

TOOLS/EQUIPMENT

- 1 or 2 baking sheets
- Parchment paper
- Zip-top bag
- Wire cooling rack or kitchen towel

½ cup (1 stick) unsalted butter, at room temperature

¾ cup brown sugar

1 large egg

½ teaspoon vanilla extract

1 cup all-purpose flour

½ teaspoon baking soda

½ teaspoon salt

4 or 5 sheets of graham crackers, divided

½ cup mini marshmallows

¾ cup chocolate chips

PREHEAT YOUR OVEN TO 350°F.

Line the baking sheets with parchment paper.

MIX THE DOUGH.

In a large mixing bowl, cream together the butter and brown sugar. Add the egg and vanilla and mix again. In a medium mixing bowl, combine the flour, baking soda, and salt and mix. Add the dry ingredients to the wet ingredients and mix, forming a dough.

FOLD IN THE GRAHAM CRACKERS AND CHOCOLATE CHIPS.

Add 3 sheets of graham crackers to a zip-top bag. With your hands, gently crush the graham crackers. Leave some bits still in medium pieces, about the size of your pinky. You should have about ¾ cup. Fold the graham cracker bits and chocolate chips into the batter.

BAKE THE COOKIES.

Scoop 2 tablespoons of dough into balls and place 6 dough balls on each baking sheet. Bake for 10 to 12 minutes.

› CONTINUED

Trouble-shooting: Don't fold the marshmallows into the batter—press them in at the end. Mini marshmallows mixed into the dough would melt too fast, causing the marshmallow to leak onto your pan and even burn.

ADD MARSHMALLOWS AND OTHER DECORATIONS.
While the cookies are baking, add 1 or 2 sheets of graham crackers to a zip-top bag. With your hands, gently crush the graham crackers. Remove the cookies from the oven and place on a pot holder. While the cookies are still warm, quickly and gently press 3 or 4 mini marshmallows into each cookie. Work fast and be careful with the hot pan! Press in chocolate chips and the graham cracker chunks after adding marshmallows.

COOL THE COOKIES BEFORE STORING.
Allow the cookies to cool on the pan for 1 to 2 minutes. Transfer the cookies to a wire rack or a clean kitchen towel to fully cool.

Shark Attack Cheesecakes

PREP TIME: 45 minutes | **BAKE TIME:** no bake | **YIELD:** 4 dessert jars

Shark Week is a long-running TV event that has families and friends gathering around to watch and learn about sharks every summer. Obsessed with these toothy giants? This fin-filled dessert is the perfect way to celebrate.

TOOLS/EQUIPMENT

- Electric mixer or stand mixer
- 2 strong plastic zip-top bags
- 4 clear jars (4-ounce or 6-ounce, such as small mason jars)
- 1 piece of paper
- Black marker
- Baking sheet
- Parchment paper

½ cup graham cracker crumbs (about 4 sheets)

2 tablespoons unsalted butter, melted

1 cup candy melts in blue, teal, gray, or white

2 tablespoons powdered sugar

1 cup heavy (whipping) cream

FREEZE THE BOWL AND BEATERS.
Place your large mixing bowl and whisk attachment or beaters in the freezer. This will be for making your whipped cream.

MAKE THE GRAHAM CRACKER CRUST.
Place the graham crackers in a zip-top bag. With your hands, gently crush the crackers into crumbs. Mix together the graham cracker crumbs and melted butter. Drop spoonfuls of the graham cracker mixture evenly between the glass jars and press down.

MAKE THE SHARK FINS.
On a piece of paper, draw four shark fins with a black marker. The bottom of the fin should be about 1 inch across and should fit into the glass jar. Put the paper on a baking sheet as your pattern and place parchment paper on top. Melt the candy melts according to the package instructions and spoon into a zip-top bag. Snip a corner of the bag and use the liquid melts to draw and fill in the shark fins on the parchment paper. Place the fins in the freezer to harden.

› CONTINUED

Food coloring
8 ounces cream cheese,
    at room temperature
2 tablespoons
    granulated sugar
1 teaspoon fresh
    lemon juice
½ teaspoon
    vanilla extract
4 tablespoons red
    jam (strawberry,
    raspberry, etc.)

MAKE THE WHIPPED CREAM.

Remove the mixing bowl from the freezer and add the powdered sugar and whipping cream. Mix with a mixer for 4 to 5 minutes, or until the mixture starts to form peaks—like a mountain made of fluffy whipped cream. Watch carefully—if you whip your cream too long, it will turn into butter. Set ½ cup of whipped cream aside and color it blue with food coloring.

MIX THE CHEESECAKE.

In a large mixing bowl with an electric mixer, or in the bowl of a stand mixer, add the cream cheese and beat for 2 to 3 minutes. Next add the white whipped cream (not the smaller blue one!), granulated sugar, lemon juice, and vanilla, then beat together for an additional minute to make a spreadable cheesecake.

LAYER THE SHARK CHEESECAKE IN THE JARS.

Use half of the cheesecake mixture and add a spoonful to each jar. Add a small spoonful of red jam, then the rest of the white cheesecake, then top with blue whipped cream in each jar. Chill in the refrigerator for at least 15 minutes, then pop the candy shark fins on top before you eat.

Helpful Hint: This dessert is easy to make ahead and will hold up well in the refrigerator for a few days if you cover the jars tightly with a lid or plastic wrap and a rubber band.

Shark Attack
Cheesecakes,
page 65

Brownie à la Mode Cupcakes

PREP TIME: 20 minutes, plus 20 minutes to chill | **BAKE TIME:** 12 to 14 minutes
YIELD: 12 brownies

Make Father's Day extra sweet—just add ice cream and make the perfect brownies à la mode (*à la mode* means "with ice cream")! Our family loves ice cream, and this dessert gives us many choices to pick everyone's favorite flavors and toppings. Having your ice cream be a little soft makes it much easier to spread, so make sure to take it out of the freezer and let it sit on the counter before you need it. Store any extras in the freezer, if they last that long!

TOOLS/EQUIPMENT
- Muffin pan
- Cupcake liners (optional)
- Wire cooling rack or kitchen towel

FOR THE BROWNIES
Cooking oil spray, for greasing the pan (optional)

2 large eggs

¼ cup (½ stick) unsalted butter, melted

¼ cup brown sugar

¼ cup granulated sugar

½ teaspoon vanilla extract

¼ cup all-purpose flour

¼ cup unsweetened cocoa powder

¼ teaspoon salt

½ cup white chocolate chips

2 cups ice cream, slightly softened

PREHEAT THE OVEN TO 350°F.
Line the muffin pan with cupcake liners or spray lightly with cooking oil spray.

MIX THE BROWNIE BATTER.
Beat the eggs in a large bowl, then add the melted butter, brown sugar, granulated sugar, and vanilla and mix. In a medium bowl, mix the flour, cocoa, and salt until they are combined. Add the dry ingredients to the wet ingredients and mix. Fold in the white chocolate chips.

BAKE THE BROWNIES.
Split the batter evenly among 12 muffin cups, about 1½ tablespoons of batter per muffin cup. Bake for 12 to 14 minutes, until fudgy in the middle but not raw. Carefully and quickly remove the brownies from the pan to avoid overbaking and let them cool on a wire rack.

TOP THE BROWNIES WITH ICE CREAM.
Place the brownies back in the cool muffin pan. Top each brownie with ice cream, smoothing with a spoon.

DECORATE AND FREEZE THE BROWNIES.

If desired, add sprinkles, mini chocolate chips, nuts, chocolate syrup, or caramel sauce—use your family's favorite. Freeze the brownies in the freezer for at least 20 minutes to firm them up.

TOP BROWNIES WITH WHIPPED CREAM AND A CHERRY, THEN EAT!

Remove the brownies from the freezer (it's OK to do a little dance, too!). Add whipped cream (for home-made whipped cream, make a half batch from the Cool Strawberry and Chocolate Icebox Cake on page 75) and a cherry!

World Series All-Star
Pull-Apart Cake,
page 71

World Series All-Star Pull-Apart Cake

PREP TIME: 1 hour | **BAKE TIME:** 15 to 17 minutes | **YIELD:** 28 to 30 cupcakes

Share a treat with the team on game day! This pull-apart baseball cupcake cake is perfect for celebrating after a game, at the end of the season, or as a surprise. Sneak the team color inside the cupcakes for extra fun. Decorate the baseball with laces—but maybe not all 108 stitches a real baseball has!

TOOLS/EQUIPMENT

- Muffin pan
- Cupcake liners
- Electric mixer or stand mixer
- Toothpick
- Wire cooling rack or kitchen towel
- 2 piping bags or strong plastic zip-top bags
- 1M piping tip (optional)

FOR THE CAKE

1 cup (2 sticks) unsalted butter, at room temperature
1½ cups granulated sugar
4 large eggs
1½ tablespoons vanilla extract
1 cup yogurt
2⅔ cups all-purpose flour
2½ teaspoons baking powder
½ teaspoon salt

PREHEAT THE OVEN TO 350°F.
Line the muffin pan with cupcake liners.

MIX THE CUPCAKE BATTER.
In a large mixing bowl with an electric mixer or in the bowl of a stand mixer, cream together 1 cup of butter and granulated sugar for 2 to 3 minutes. Beat the eggs in a small bowl, then mix them into the butter-sugar mixture. Add 1½ tablespoons of vanilla and the yogurt and mix well again. In a medium mixing bowl, combine the flour, baking powder, and salt. Add your dry ingredients to the wet ingredients and mix until a batter forms.

BAKE THE CUPCAKES.
Fill each cupcake liner about two-thirds full with batter. Bake for 15 to 17 minutes, or until a toothpick inserted in the center of a cupcake comes out clean. Take the cupcakes out of the pan and put them on a wire rack or a towel to cool.

MIX UP THE CREAM CHEESE FROSTING.
In a large clean mixing bowl with an electric mixer or in the bowl of a stand mixer, beat 1½ cups of butter for 5 minutes. The butter will turn a paler color. Scrape down the sides of the bowl with a spatula, then add the cream cheese and beat for 1 to 2 minutes. Add the powdered sugar slowly, 1 cup at a time, mixing until fluffy. Add 2 teaspoons of vanilla and mix.

› CONTINUED

FOR THE CREAM CHEESE FROSTING AND DECORATIONS

1½ cups (3 sticks) unsalted butter, at room temperature

12 ounces cream cheese (about a block and a half), at room temperature

6 cups powdered sugar

2 teaspoons vanilla extract

Food coloring, in team colors

4 pieces red licorice (like Twizzlers)

Helpful Hint:

Before frosting, put your cupcakes on your platter to make sure there's enough room.

FILL THE CUPCAKES WITH FROSTING IN THE TEAM COLOR.

Set aside 1 cup of frosting and color it with food coloring. Use the frosting advice on page 19 to fill a bag with the colored frosting. Cut small holes in the tops of the cupcakes about the size of a quarter and set aside the tops. (You can also use a clean metal piping tip to cut the hole.) Fill the center of the cupcake with frosting (not too full!), then close it again with the cake.

ARRANGE THE CUPCAKES TO MAKE A CAKE.

Line 5 cupcakes across your cake platter. Then above and below add a row of 4 cupcakes, and then a row of 3 cupcakes. Keep the cupcakes close together. Any extra cupcakes can be frosted separately and made into mini baseballs to put around the cake.

FROST AND DECORATE CUPCAKES.

Follow the instructions on page 19 to put your frosting in a piping bag or zip-top bag. If you have piping tips, I recommend using a 1M. Pipe circles of frosting on each of your cupcakes, starting in the center and spiraling to the outside of each cupcake.

DECORATE THE BASEBALLS WITH LACES.

Take 2 pieces of licorice and cut them each into 4 even pieces. Lay 2 long pieces of licorice on the cupcakes as the laces of the baseball. Use the smaller pieces of licorice to make the baseball stitches. Decorate extra cupcakes with smaller pieces of licorice for laces.

Watermelon Pizza Cookie Cake

PREP TIME: 30 minutes | **BAKE TIME:** 18 to 20 minutes | **YIELD:** 8 to 10 slices

Eating fresh fruit in the summer is delicious, and it's so yummy on a giant cookie! Serve this cookie cake up for a backyard BBQ, a day at the lake, or for a pool party. This extra-sweet watermelon cookie is full of fluffy cream cheese frosting, sugar cookie, and lots of fresh fruit. Look for the best berries that are bright red and smell fruity to decorate with.

TOOLS/EQUIPMENT

- Baking sheet
- Parchment paper
- Electric mixer or stand mixer
- Rolling pin
- 2 chopsticks (optional)
- 9-inch plate

FOR THE COOKIE CAKE

½ cup (1 stick) unsalted butter, cold
½ cup granulated sugar
¼ teaspoon vanilla extract
1 large egg, cold
1½ cups all-purpose flour, plus more for rolling
¼ teaspoon salt

FOR THE FROSTING

1 cup (2 sticks) unsalted butter, at room temperature
8 ounces cream cheese, at room temperature
4 cups powdered sugar
2 teaspoons vanilla extract

PREHEAT THE OVEN TO 350°F.

Line the baking sheet with parchment paper.

MIX THE COOKIE DOUGH.

Slice 1 butter stick into 10 to 12 pieces and let it sit on the counter for 5 minutes. In a large mixing bowl with a strong wooden spoon, or in the bowl of a stand mixer, cream the butter pieces and granulated sugar together. Add ¼ teaspoon of vanilla and the egg to the bowl and mix until smooth. Add the flour and salt and cut the butter mixture into the flour. You should be able to squeeze your dough together like Play-Doh. If your dough is too dry or feels more like sand, add 1 tablespoon of water.

ROLL OUT THE COOKIE DOUGH FLAT.

Lightly flour a clean counter and the rolling pin. Roll out your dough, adding flour to the top of it. Lay two chopsticks on either side of your dough. Roll until it is about ⅜ inch thick, a little thicker than a chopstick. Trace the plate on the dough to make a giant round cookie. Slide the giant cookie onto the baking sheet. Chill the dough for about 20 minutes.

› CONTINUED

FOR THE DECORATIONS

1 cup green grapes,
    sliced in half
1 cup strawberries, cut
    into thin slices
¼ cup chocolate chips

BAKE THE COOKIE.

Bake the cookie for 18 to 20 minutes, until it's light brown on the bottom but still pale and feels like it has a dry skin across the top if you tap it with a finger (not doughy). Using the parchment paper, slide the cookie off the baking sheet and allow it to cool.

MAKE THE CREAM CHEESE FROSTING.

In a large bowl with an electric mixer or in the bowl of a stand mixer, whip 1 cup of room-temperature butter on medium speed for 4 to 5 minutes. Scrape down the sides of the bowl and add the cream cheese, mixing to combine. Scrape down the bowl again and add the powdered sugar 1 cup at a time, mixing well. Add 2 teaspoons of vanilla and mix for 1 minute more.

DECORATE THE COOKIE.

Frost the cookie cake with all the frosting. Put a line of sliced grapes in a ring around the entire outside of the cookie. Decorate the middle with slices of strawberries and then top with chocolate chips to look like watermelon seeds. Chill the cookie in the refrigerator until time to serve, then slice and enjoy.

Did You Know? Strawberries aren't technically berries, because the fruit doesn't surround the seeds—but watermelon is!

Cool Strawberry and Chocolate Icebox Cake

PREP TIME: 20 minutes | **BAKE TIME:** no bake | **YIELD:** 12 slices

When summertime gets hot, a cold dessert like this strawberry-chocolate icebox cake brings everyone running. It's the perfect dessert for hot summer backyard BBQs. This cake is a combo of gooey chocolate, fluffy whipped cream, and fresh strawberries. You can also swap different types of berries, add caramel, drizzle with warmed peanut butter, or even add chopped nuts for your own creative cake!

TOOLS/EQUIPMENT

- Electric mixer or stand mixer
- Microwave
- Whisk
- 8-by-11-inch baking pan
- Piping bag or strong plastic zip-top bag

16 ounces strawberries (1 clamshell)

4½ cups cold heavy (whipping) cream, divided

1 cup powdered sugar

2 teaspoons vanilla extract

½ cup semisweet chocolate chips

8 ounces graham crackers (about 2 sleeves)

CHILL THE WHIPPED CREAM MIXING BOWL.

Place a large mixing bowl and your beaters or whisk attachment in the freezer for 10 minutes to chill.

PREP THE STRAWBERRIES.

Rinse and dry your strawberries. Slice the tops off the berries, and then cut them into ¼-inch slices.

MAKE THE WHIPPED CREAM.

Add 4 cups of cold heavy whipping cream to the cold mixing bowl. With a mixer, whip for 2 to 3 minutes, until the liquid starts to grow in size. Add the powdered sugar slowly, mixing it into the cream. Soft peaks (like the shape of a mountain) will begin to form, and you will be able to swirl a spoon through the cream and the swirl will hold. Mix in the vanilla. Be careful not to overwhip the whipped cream, as it will separate, and butter will begin to form.

MELT THE CHOCOLATE TO MAKE GANACHE.

Place the chocolate chips in a medium glass bowl. In another medium glass bowl, heat the remaining ½ cup of heavy whipping cream in the microwave until it just begins to boil, about 1 minute. Pour the cream over the chocolate and whisk until the chocolate is smooth, 2 to 3 minutes.

› CONTINUED

Did You Know?

Strawberries are grown in every single US state and every Canadian province! You likely don't have to go far to find fresh berries.

PREP THE WHIPPED CREAM.

Add a thin layer of whipped cream in the bottom of your pan, spreading it with a spatula. Following the instructions on page 19, add the rest of your whipped cream to a piping bag or zip-top bag.

LAYER THE INGREDIENTS IN THE PAN AND CHILL.

On top of the whipped cream in the pan, add a layer of graham crackers. Add dollops of whipped cream between the size of a nickel and a quarter on each graham cracker. Layer on half of the strawberries, then drizzle half of the chocolate ganache. Repeat with a second layer of graham crackers, whipped cream, strawberries, and chocolate. Chill in the freezer for at least 30 minutes or until you're ready to eat dessert.

Bursting Blueberry Mini Galettes (Pies!)

PREP TIME: 20 minutes | **BAKE TIME:** 13 to 15 minutes | **YIELD:** 4 pastries

In the summer, big, ripe, juicy blueberries are another family favorite for breakfast or snacks. We always bring home a massive haul of blueberries and spend time together turning the berries into all kinds of treats. These galettes may sound a little fancy, but they're simply a fast and easy way to make a mini pie. The best part is these mini pies can double as dessert or breakfast!

TOOLS/EQUIPMENT

- Baking sheet
- Parchment paper
- Cutting board
- Silicone brush
- Wire cooling rack or kitchen towel

¼ cup sugar, plus more for sprinkling

1 tablespoon fresh lemon juice

½ teaspoon vanilla extract

Pinch salt

1 cup blueberries

1 sheet frozen puff pastry, thawed to package instructions

1 to 2 tablespoons all-purpose flour (optional)

1 large egg

1 tablespoon water

PREHEAT THE OVEN TO 425°F.
Line the baking sheet with parchment paper.

MIX THE BLUEBERRY FILLING.
In a large mixing bowl, combine the sugar, lemon juice, vanilla, and salt. (To grab a pinch of salt, pour a little salt in one hand, and with your other, pinch a little salt between your pointer finger and thumb.) Then fold the blueberries into your sugar mixture and set aside.

SLICE THE PUFF PASTRY DOUGH.
Unroll the puff pastry dough on a cutting board, sprinkling a light dusting of flour under the dough if it starts to stick. Cut the puff pastry into 4 equal squares. Trim and round the corners just a little for each square of dough, making them the same shape as an app icon.

PREPARE THE DOUGH FOR THE FILLING.
Beat the egg with the water. This is called an egg wash. It's used to help pastries and bread get a brown crust. Using a silicone brush, brush the egg wash around the outside of each pastry square. Place ¼ cup of blueberry mixture in the middle of each square.

› CONTINUED

Try Instead:
Any flavor of berry, and many other summery fruits, can be substituted for blueberries in this galette. Try strawberries, raspberries, peaches, plums, or even apples sprinkled with a little cinnamon. Just skip melons—they don't bake well!

FOLD THE DOUGH AND PRESS IT FIRMLY TOGETHER.
Fold the outside edge of the dough in, pressing with a spoon to make an edge crust like a pizza crust. Turn the galette and keep folding in the edge around the whole outside. The folds should be about ½ inch of dough. Repeat this for all 4 galettes.

BAKE THE GALETTES.
Using a silicone brush, brush the entire crust of the galettes with the egg mixture. Sprinkle the edges of your galettes with a little sugar. Bake in the oven for 13 to 15 minutes, or until the galettes begin to turn a light golden-brown color on the edges. Let the galettes cool on a towel or wire rack and enjoy!

Bursting Blueberry
Mini Galettes (Pies!),
page 77

Day of the Dead
Sugar Skull Cookies,
page 92

4 fall

Fall is the season for being cozy! In this chapter, you can celebrate pumpkins, apples, colored leaves, and maple. Whether you're looking for something for Halloween, Day of the Dead, or Diwali, you'll find yummy treats in this chapter for celebrating in the fall.

Spooky Ghost
Double-Chocolate Cupcakes

PREP TIME: 30 minutes | **BAKE TIME:** 15 to 17 minutes | **YIELD:** 12 to 14 cupcakes

What do ghosts eat for dinner? Spook-ghetti! After that, they'll be looking for these double-chocolate cupcakes for dessert. Bring these cupcakes to a Halloween party to share with all of your favorite boos and ghouls. The ghost marshmallows are dipped in white chocolate to give them a delicious crunch, and the cupcakes are SO chocolatey. Yum!

TOOLS/EQUIPMENT

- Muffin pan
- Cupcake liners
- 15 toothpicks
- Wire cooling rack or kitchen towel
- Electric mixer or stand mixer
- Microwave
- Piping bags or strong plastic zip-top bags
- Parchment paper

FOR THE CUPCAKES

2 large eggs
¾ cup granulated sugar
½ cup yogurt
½ cup oil
2 teaspoons vanilla extract
1 cup all-purpose flour
½ cup unsweetened cocoa powder
1¼ teaspoons baking powder
½ teaspoon baking soda
½ teaspoon salt
2 tablespoons milk

PREHEAT THE OVEN TO 350°F.

Line your muffin pan with cupcake liners.

MIX THE CUPCAKE BATTER.

In a large mixing bowl, beat the eggs. Then add the granulated sugar, yogurt, oil, and 2 teaspoons of vanilla and mix well. In a medium mixing bowl, mix together the flour, cocoa, baking powder, baking soda, and salt until well combined. Add the flour mixture to the wet ingredients and mix until all the dry ingredients are mixed in. Mix in the milk to thin the batter.

BAKE THE CUPCAKES.

Fill each cupcake liner about two-thirds full with batter. Bake for 15 to 17 minutes, or until a toothpick inserted in the center of a cupcake comes out clean. Take the cupcakes out of the muffin pan when they're cool enough to handle and cool them on a towel or wire rack.

FOR THE CHOCOLATE–CREAM CHEESE FROSTING

½ cup (1 stick) unsalted butter, at room temperature
4 ounces cream cheese, at room temperature
1 teaspoon vanilla extract
2 cups powdered sugar
1 cup chocolate chips

FOR THE DECORATIONS

Black and orange sprinkles (optional)
14 large marshmallows
1 cup white candy melts
28 candy eyeballs
14 chocolate chips
Candy pumpkins (optional)

MAKE THE CHOCOLATE FROSTING.

In a clean large mixing bowl with an electric mixer or in the bowl of a stand mixer, add the butter and beat on medium speed for 5 minutes. The butter will turn a paler color. Scrape down the sides of the bowl with a spatula, then add the cream cheese and vanilla and whip together for 1 to 2 minutes. Add the powdered sugar, ½ cup at a time, mixing well in between each addition. In a clean, dry bowl, put 1 cup of chocolate chips. Melt in the microwave at half power, heating for 30 seconds at a time, stirring each time until melted. Fold the chocolate into your frosting and mix well while still warm.

FROST THE CUPCAKES.

Follow the instructions on page 19 to put your frosting in a piping bag or zip-top bag. Frost the cupcakes by making a small swirl of frosting in the middle of the cupcake. Move to the outer edge of the cupcake, working in circles, and then move back up toward the center to make a swirly top. Add sprinkles to the top (if desired).

› CONTINUED

Try Instead: These cupcakes look extra fun if you place a candy pumpkin next to each ghoul. Also try small candy bones if you can find them. Even big candy eyes can be a lot of fun!

DECORATE THE CUPCAKES WITH MARSHMALLOW GHOSTS.

Place each marshmallow on a toothpick. Put the candy melts in a bowl and melt according to package instructions. Working quickly and holding the toothpick and the bottom of the marshmallow, dip the top of the marshmallow in the white chocolate, then attach 2 candy eyes and set them on a piece of parchment paper. Repeat for all the ghosts, wiping your hands on a towel as needed. Once firm, remove the toothpick and place the ghosts gently on top of the cupcake in the frosting. You can add a chocolate chip mouth, pushing the pointy end of the chocolate chip into the marshmallows.

Trick-or-Treat Candy
Overload Brownies,
page 86

Trick-or-Treat Candy Overload Brownies

PREP TIME: 30 minutes | **BAKE TIME:** 30 to 35 minutes | **YIELD:** 10 to 12 brownies

This brownie came out of the ultimate Halloween question—what do I do with all this candy? Use all your favorite chocolate candies, then decorate the top of the brownies with a drizzle of cheesecake topping, candy eyeballs, and—you guessed it—more candy!

TOOLS/EQUIPMENT

- 8- or 9-inch square baking pan
- Parchment paper
- Whisk
- Electric mixer or stand mixer
- Toothpick

Oil, for greasing the pan
3 large eggs, plus
    1 egg yolk
½ cup (1 stick) unsalted
    butter, melted
½ cup brown sugar
¾ cup granulated
    sugar, divided
1 teaspoon vanilla extract
½ cup all-purpose flour
½ cup unsweetened
    cocoa powder
¼ teaspoon salt
1 cup chopped chocolate
    Halloween candy, plus
    more for decorating
4 ounces cream cheese,
    at room temperature
Food coloring
Candy eyes (optional)

PREHEAT THE OVEN TO 350°F.
Line the baking pan with parchment paper and oil the sides of the pan well. Cut the parchment paper to be the same size as the pan by tracing the pan.

MIX THE BATTER FOR THE BROWNIES.
Whisk 3 eggs in a medium mixing bowl. Add the melted butter, brown sugar, ½ cup of granulated sugar, and vanilla and mix until well combined. In another medium bowl, combine the flour, cocoa, and salt and mix well. Add the dry mixture to your wet ingredients and mix together with a whisk. Fold 1 cup of chopped chocolate candy into the batter.

MAKE THE CHEESECAKE SWIRL FOR THE TOPPING.
In a large bowl with an electric mixer or in the bowl of a stand mixer, whip the cream cheese for 1 to 2 minutes. Add the egg yolk to your cream cheese mixture. (To separate the yolk, crack an egg over a bowl, gently catching the egg yolk with the shell and letting the egg white drip down into the bowl. The egg white can be used for another recipe like the Gooey Passover Double-Chocolate Flourless Cookies on page 36.) Add the remaining ¼ cup of granulated sugar and mix. Add food coloring to make the mixture a Halloween color. I used 5 drops of yellow and 1 drop of red food coloring to make orange.

Trouble-shooting: These brownies are delicious, but it can sometimes be tough to tell if they are cooked all the way. Ask an adult to help you pick up the hot pan with oven mitts and slowly tip the pan back and forth just a little. Watch to see if the center of the dough moves. If it moves, the brownies need to cook more!

BAKE THE BROWNIES.

Add the brownie batter to the pan lined with parchment and spread evenly using a silicone spatula. Add spoonfuls of the cream cheese mixture spread out over the brownie batter. Drag a butter knife through the cream cheese just a little, creating brownie and cream cheese swirls across the top. Bake for 30 to 35 minutes, until a toothpick inserted in the center comes out clean. The brownie should be fudgy inside but not raw.

ADD MORE CANDY TO THE BROWNIES.

While the brownies are baking, arrange your remaining chopped chocolate candy in small bowls. When the brownies have finished but are still warm, gently push small chunks of chocolate candy, single or pairs of candy eyes, and any other candies or chocolates on top. Let the brownies cool completely before removing them from the pan and enjoying.

Pumpkin Pie Dumplings

PREP TIME: 25 minutes | **BAKE TIME:** 15 to 17 minutes | **YIELD:** 9 dumplings

When the season turns to fall, many people start thinking about apples, leaves, and pumpkin pie. Pumpkin pie flavor has worked its way into so many desserts these days and almost always has a place at the Thanksgiving table. These little pumpkin dumplings are a cute mini popover version of a full pie. Use dough scraps to make pumpkin faces or add a little powdered sugar on top as the finishing touch.

TOOLS/EQUIPMENT

- Muffin pan
- Whisk
- Cutting board
- Silicone brush
- 3-inch pumpkin or round cookie cutter
- Sifter or screen with a fine mesh (optional)

Oil, for greasing the pan
1 large egg
2 tablespoons mashed pumpkin
1 tablespoon yogurt
2 tablespoons brown sugar
½ teaspoon cinnamon
¼ teaspoon nutmeg
Flour, for dusting the work surface
2 sheets frozen puff pastry dough, thawed to package instructions
1 tablespoon water
Powdered sugar, for sprinkling (optional)

PREHEAT THE OVEN TO 400°F.
Coat the muffin pan lightly with oil.

SEPARATE THE EGG.
Over a small bowl, crack the egg. Separate the yolk from the white by placing the yolk into your hands and letting the egg white drip down into the small bowl. Be careful not to break the yolk. Set aside the egg white. Put the yolk in a large bowl and beat it with a whisk.

MAKE THE PUMPKIN PIE FILLING.
Add the pumpkin, yogurt, brown sugar, cinnamon, and nutmeg to the bowl with the egg yolk. Mix until well combined.

PREPARE THE PUFF PASTRY DOUGH AND ASSEMBLE THE DUMPLINGS.
On a floured cutting board, gently unroll a piece of puff pastry. Slice the pastry into 9 equal pieces. Place a piece of puff pastry in each muffin cup. With a fork, prick the center of each dough four or five times. Add the water to the egg white and mix to make an egg wash, then brush each piece of dough with egg wash using a silicone brush. Fill each cup of dough with about 1½ tablespoons of the pumpkin filling.

CUT OUT THE PUMPKIN TOPS FROM THE PUFF PASTRY.
Using a 3-inch pumpkin cookie cutter, cut 9 pumpkins out of the second piece of puff pastry dough on your cutting board (a 3-inch circle also works). Brush one side of the pumpkin well with the egg wash and press the egg side down gently on top of each pumpkin dumpling. Brush the top of each pumpkin with more egg wash. If you'd like to make jack-o'-lantern eyes, noses, and mouths, cut them out of the puff pastry scraps and attach to the tops with the egg wash, then brush the top with egg wash.

BAKE THE PUMPKIN PIE DUMPLINGS.
Bake the pumpkin pie dumplings for 15 to 17 minutes, until golden brown on top and not raw inside. The dumplings will puff up a lot. After a few minutes, carefully remove them from the muffin pans with a thin spatula or butter knife. Try not to poke into the dumplings. Decorate with powdered sugar (if using) by sprinkling the sugar through a sifter, and enjoy!

Candy Corn
Magic Cookies,
page 91

Candy Corn Magic Cookies

PREP TIME: 15 minutes | **BAKE TIME:** 11 to 13 minutes | **YIELD:** 18 or 19 cookies

Candy corn is the second most popular Halloween candy, right behind chocolate, and it's one of my favorites! You can find candy corn in colors for Christmas, Valentine's Day, and more. Whatever holiday you make these cookies for, they will be a hit!

TOOLS/EQUIPMENT

- 1 or 2 baking sheets
- Parchment paper
- Cookie scoop (optional)

½ cup (1 stick) unsalted butter, at room temperature
½ cup brown sugar
¼ cup granulated sugar
1 large egg
½ teaspoon vanilla extract
1½ cups all-purpose flour
½ teaspoon baking soda
¼ teaspoon salt
½ cup white chocolate chips, plus more for decorating
½ cup candy corn

Did You Know?

The flavor of candy corn is a mixture of vanilla, marshmallow, and a buttery flavor.

PREHEAT THE OVEN TO 350°F.
Line the baking sheets with parchment paper.

MIX THE WET INGREDIENTS.
In a large mixing bowl, cream together the butter, brown sugar, and granulated sugar until smooth. Add the egg and vanilla, mixing until combined.

MIX THE DRY INGREDIENTS AND MAKE A COOKIE DOUGH.
In a medium bowl, mix together the flour, baking soda, and salt. Add the flour mixture to the wet ingredients and mix until combined. Fold the white chocolate chips into the batter.

BAKE THE COOKIES.
Using a cookie scoop or a tablespoon, scoop out 2 tablespoons of dough and roll into a ball. Place 6 balls on each baking sheet, leaving about 2 inches in between each. Bake for 11 to 13 minutes, until they are gooey in the center but no longer raw.

ADD CANDY CORN TO THE TOPS OF THE COOKIES.
Remove the cookies from the oven and place your pan on a pot holder. While the cookies are still hot, press 3 or 4 candy corn pieces into each cookie. Work fast while the cookies are still hot, but be careful not to touch the pan! Allow the cookies to cool, and enjoy.

Day of the Dead Sugar Skull Cookies

PREP TIME: 60 minutes | **BAKE TIME:** 11 to 12 minutes | **YIELD:** 18 cookies

One of the most recognized symbols of Day of the Dead (Día de los Muertos) is the beautifully decorated sugar skulls created to honor and celebrate family members. Create your own decorations on your cookie skulls, such as flowers, swirls, and bright colors. You can show appreciation for someone you care about by giving them one of your beautifully decorated cookies! This recipe calls for meringue powder, which can be found at most craft stores in the decorating section, but you can also use the buttercream found on page 52.

TOOLS/EQUIPMENT

- 2 baking sheets
- Parchment paper
- Stand mixer (optional)
- Rolling pin
- 2 chopsticks (optional)
- Skull cookie cutter or 3½-inch round cookie cutter
- Wire cooling rack or kitchen towel
- Toothpicks (optional)

FOR THE COOKIES

1 cup (2 sticks) unsalted butter, cold
1 cup granulated sugar
4 large eggs, cold
2 teaspoons vanilla extract
3 cups all-purpose flour, plus more for rolling
⅔ cup unsweetened cocoa powder
½ teaspoon baking powder
¼ teaspoon salt

PREHEAT THE OVEN TO 350°F.
Line the baking sheets with parchment paper.

CREAM THE BUTTER AND SUGAR AND MIX THE WET INGREDIENTS.
Slice each butter stick into 10 to 12 pieces. Set the butter on the counter for about 5 minutes, which softens it a little while keeping it cold. In a large mixing bowl with a strong wooden spoon or in the bowl of your stand mixer, cream the butter pieces with the granulated sugar. Add the eggs and 2 teaspoons of vanilla, then mix just until you see no more large chunks of butter.

MAKE THE CHOCOLATE COOKIE DOUGH.
In a separate bowl, mix together 3 cups of flour, the cocoa powder, baking powder, and salt. With a wooden spoon, mix the dry ingredients with the wet ingredients in the larger bowl until the dough comes together. (Don't try mixing this part of the dough with an electric hand mixer—the dough is very thick and may break your mixer!) You should be able to squeeze your dough together like Play-Doh.

FOR THE WHITE BASE ICING

2 cups powdered sugar
¼ cup water
2 tablespoons
    meringue powder
1 teaspoon vanilla extract

FOR EACH DECORATIVE COLORED ICING

1 cup powdered sugar
1 tablespoon
    meringue powder
2 tablespoons water
Food coloring
    assortment (gel
    food coloring makes
    brighter colors)

FOR THE DECORATIONS

Sprinkles
Candies

CUT OUT THE SKULL COOKIES.

Lightly flour a clean counter and the rolling pin. Roll out your dough, adding flour to the top of it. Lay two chopsticks on either side of your dough. Roll until it is about ⅜ inch thick, a little thicker than a chopstick. Using your cookie cutter, cut out cookies. Reroll any scraps into a ball, then roll out again to cut more cookies, repeating until you can't cut any more.

BAKE THE COOKIES.

Bake the cookies for 11 to 12 minutes. The cookies should still be a little chewy inside. If you cook them too long, they start to taste more like brownie brittle! Remove the cookies and cool them on a wire rack or towel so they don't keep cooking on the hot pan.

MAKE THE BASE ICING.

In a small bowl, add the powdered sugar, ¼ cup of water, 2 tablespoons of meringue powder, and 1 teaspoon of vanilla and mix well.

› CONTINUED

Helpful Hint: Sugar skulls are super decorative, so check out some pictures of them online for more decoration inspiration. You can choose to make the entire skull white, blue, pink, green, or whatever color you like.

MAKE THE DECORATIVE COLORED ICING.

Mix up each color of icing by mixing together 1 cup of powdered sugar, 2 tablespoons of water, 1 tablespoon of meringue powder, ½ teaspoon of vanilla, and gel food coloring. Add the icing to a piping bag as explained on page 19.

DIP AND DECORATE THE COOKIES.

Dip each cookie in white icing. Place the cookies in the refrigerator for about 15 minutes to help the white icing set. Then use your colored icing to pipe colorful decorations onto the cookies and use any candies or sprinkles to help add color and fun. Create daisies at the eyes, a swirl on each cheek, a few colored decorative dots on the forehead, and a toothy grin. Use a toothpick to smooth your design as needed. Place the cookies back in the refrigerator for a few minutes to set the colored icing, then enjoy the cookies!

Fudgy Diwali Chocolate Burfi

PREP TIME: 15 minutes, plus 60 minutes to chill | **COOK TIME:** 10 minutes | **YIELD:** 12 pieces

Different flavors of burfi are a traditional dessert of Diwali's five-day festival of lights. A sweet candy creation similar to fudge, it's made from milk and the name literally means "snow." Many flavors of burfi are white or contain a snow-white layer. Rose water, cardamom, and coconut are all common flavors, along with the ever-popular chocolate version. This is an adapted version of the delicious Indian treat.

TOOLS/EQUIPMENT

- Medium saucepan
- Whisk (optional)
- 8- or 9-inch square baking pan
- Parchment paper

2 tablespoons ghee or unsalted butter

1 cup powdered milk

½ cup unsweetened cocoa powder

14 ounces sweetened condensed milk

¼ teaspoon cardamom, or ½ teaspoon vanilla extract

½ cup chopped pistachios or walnuts

HEAT THE INGREDIENTS.

In a medium saucepan, heat the ghee or butter over medium heat and allow to melt completely. Add the powdered milk and cocoa powder, and stir with a wooden spoon or whisk until well mixed without clumps.

ADD CONDENSED MILK.

Add the condensed milk to the pan. (Burfi traditionally uses milk solids called *khoya*, which is milk that has been cooked for usually around 8 hours. It's not always easy to find, so we'll use sweetened condensed milk as a substitute.) Use a metal spoon to carefully get as much of the sticky condensed milk out of the can as you can. Using your wooden spoon, mix the condensed milk well into your batter.

COOK YOUR BATTER.

Continue stirring your batter in the pan over medium heat for 3 to 5 minutes, until the batter starts to become firmer. The time can vary a little between different types of powdered milk. You want your batter to go from a smooth and sticky liquid to a stickier consistency that is pulling away from the sides of the pan. It reminds me a lot of a warm taffy.

› CONTINUED

FILL YOUR PAN WITH BATTER AND DECORATE.

Line your baking pan with parchment paper. Do not skip using parchment paper or your dessert will stick! When your batter is pulling away from the sides of the pan, use a silicone spatula or a spoon greased with ghee or butter to spread it on the parchment paper in the pan. Try to make your batter as square as you can. Top with chopped pistachios or walnuts and refrigerate for 30 to 60 minutes. Your dessert should set and be fudge-like after chilling.

TRIM AND SLICE BURFI.

Once chilled, your sweet burfi should slice easily with a sharp knife. To make squares that are even, you can start by trimming the entire slab into an even square. I slice this dessert into about 12 pieces.

Apple Crisp Pizza Party

PREP TIME: 20 minutes | **BAKE TIME:** 30 to 35 minutes | **YIELD:** 8 slices

Holy moly, this Apple Crisp Pizza is one of those desserts that just stops people in their tracks. It's all the fun of pizza with gooey, buttery, fall apple flavor mixed in one! Does your family have a pizza night? We have pizza many Friday nights to end the week, and this dessert really knocked the socks off Friday. For a crowd, cut this dessert pizza into smaller squares instead of pizza slices and watch them disappear!

TOOLS/EQUIPMENT

- Baking sheet
- Parchment paper
- Rolling pin
- Silicone brush
- Pastry cutter (optional)
- Wire cooling rack or kitchen towel
- Silicone pastry brush

FOR THE DOUGH

1¼ cups self-rising flour, plus more for rolling
1 cup Greek yogurt

FOR THE APPLE FILLING

2 teaspoons cinnamon
⅓ cup granulated sugar
2 tablespoons all-purpose flour
2 green apples, cut into ¼-inch dice

PREHEAT THE OVEN TO 350°F.
Line a baking sheet with parchment paper.

MIX THE DOUGH.
In a large bowl, mix together the self-rising flour (see page 9 for more details about this special flour) and Greek yogurt until combined. Add a handful of flour to a clean kitchen counter. Place the dough ball on the counter, kneading with your hands for 1 to 2 minutes, adding more flour as needed to keep it from sticking to the counter. Flip and stretch the dough until it stretches easily like a pizza dough.

ROLL THE DOUGH WITH A ROLLING PIN.
Sprinkle flour on your rolling pin and counter so it won't stick to the dough. Roll the dough into a circle that is 9 to 10 inches across, adding more flour as needed. Make a crust around the edge by rolling in about 1 inch of dough all the way around your pizza. Carefully move the dough to the baking sheet.

MAKE THE APPLE FILLING.
In a medium bowl mix the cinnamon, granulated sugar, and 2 tablespoons of all-purpose flour. Add the apples and toss.

› CONTINUED

FOR THE CRUMBLE TOPPING

¼ cup all-purpose flour
¼ cup brown sugar
½ teaspoon cinnamon
¼ cup rolled oats
Pinch salt
3 tablespoons unsalted butter, at room temperature

PREPARE THE BUTTERY CRUMBLE TOPPING.

In a medium bowl, add ¼ cup of flour, brown sugar, cinnamon, oats, and salt, then mix well until combined. Cut your butter into small pieces. Using a pastry cutter or a fork, cut the butter into the oats mixture. Push butter through the prongs over and over again, mixing it into your dry mixture to make the crumble. This takes a few minutes, but your dry ingredients will go from being dry to crumbly looking without any dry bits at all.

LAYER AND BAKE THE APPLE PIZZA.

Spread the apple mixture on the dough evenly, keeping it off the crust edge. Next, sprinkle the oat mixture all over the apples. Place the apple pizza on the baking sheet in the oven and bake for 30 to 35 minutes, or until cooked all the way through (check the center). Enjoy!

Try Instead: This Apple Crisp Pizza is best warm and gooey! It is delicious all on its own, but to make it even fancier, top it with a drizzle of caramel, or drizzle the glaze from the Raspberry Sweetheart Rolls on page 137.

Apple Crisp
Pizza Party,
page 97

Ooey-Gooey Maple-Cinnamon French Toast Muffins

PREP TIME: 15 minutes | **BAKE TIME:** 25 to 30 minutes | **YIELD:** 12 muffins

If you find yourself with a three-day weekend, enjoy sleeping in a little, then pop these gooey maple-cinnamon French toast muffins in the oven for an easy brunch. These muffins also reheat well, so they are the perfect special breakfast to make ahead of time and enjoy before you set off for a fall hike or other adventures.

TOOLS/EQUIPMENT
- Muffin pan
- Whisk

FOR THE MUFFINS

Cooking oil spray, for greasing the pan

7 to 8 cups chewy, crusty bread, cut into ½-inch cubes

5 large eggs

½ cup milk, plus 2 tablespoons milk

½ teaspoon vanilla extract

2 tablespoons cinnamon, divided

¼ cup granulated sugar

PREHEAT THE OVEN TO 350°F.

Spray your muffin pan well with cooking oil spray.

MEASURE THE BREAD.

Fill each of the muffin cups just past full with bread. This will help you figure out how much you need. If you have a bread that is not very chewy (like sandwich bread), slice a little extra.

MIX THE EGG CUSTARD.

In a large bowl, add the eggs and whisk. Add ½ cup of milk, the vanilla, and 1 tablespoon of cinnamon, then mix until combined.

ADD THE EGG CUSTARD TO THE BREAD.

Add the bread to the large bowl and mix the bread and egg together with clean hands or a spoon. (Sometimes hands are faster!) Spoon your French toast mixture evenly in the muffin cups.

PREP AND BAKE MUFFINS.

In a medium bowl, mix the remaining 1 tablespoon of cinnamon with the granulated sugar. Sprinkle the cinnamon sugar on top of each muffin, wiping any dribbles off the pan at the end. Bake your muffins for 25 to 30 minutes.

FOR THE MAPLE GLAZE

½ cup powdered sugar
2 tablespoons milk
2 to 3 tablespoons real
maple syrup

MAKE AND DRIZZLE THE MAPLE GLAZE.

In a medium bowl, mix the powdered sugar, 2 tablespoons of milk, and the maple syrup until the sugar dissolves. Taste your glaze and add 1 tablespoon more of maple syrup only if needed. Drizzle the glaze over the muffins right before serving.

Try Instead: You can add a few extra muffins to this recipe if you have just a little extra bread—this recipe can stretch! For every 2 extra muffins you add, also add an extra egg and 2 tablespoons of milk. If adding 4 or more muffins, add an extra ½ teaspoon of cinnamon to the egg custard.

Caramel Apple Blondies

PREP TIME: 20 Minutes | **BAKE TIME:** 30 to 35 minutes | **YIELD:** 10 to 12 blondies

When the fall festivals start rolling into town, the sweet smells of apple, caramel, and cinnamon are everywhere! I bet you've seen those giant oversized caramel apples, but have you ever tried to eat one? It's a gooey-faced mess! Celebrate everything caramel apple and fall with your family right in your kitchen with these soft and gooey Caramel Apple Blondies. You'll be able to easily bite this sweet caramel apple treat.

TOOLS/EQUIPMENT

- Pencil
- 8- or 9-inch square baking pan
- Parchment paper
- Clean kitchen scissors
- Wire cooling rack or kitchen towel

Oil, for greasing the pan
3 large eggs
½ cup (1 stick) unsalted butter, melted
½ cup brown sugar
½ cup granulated sugar
1 teaspoon vanilla extract
¾ cup all-purpose flour
2 teaspoons cinnamon
¼ teaspoon salt
1 green apple, for topping
⅓ cup caramel sauce, for topping

PREHEAT THE OVEN TO 350°F.

With a pencil, trace your baking pan on a piece of parchment paper, cut out the square with clean kitchen scissors, and place it in the bottom of the baking pan. Lightly oil the sides of the pan.

MIX THE WET INGREDIENTS.

In a medium mixing bowl, whisk the eggs together until well blended and bubbly. Add the melted butter, brown sugar, granulated sugar, and vanilla and whisk until well combined.

MIX THE DRY INGREDIENTS INTO THE BATTER.

In a medium mixing bowl, combine the flour, cinnamon, and salt, then mix well. Add the dry ingredients to your wet ingredients and mix well.

FOLD THE APPLE INTO THE BATTER.

Wash and dry your apple. Grate the entire apple until you get to the core. This gives you ⅓ to ½ cup of grated apple, depending on the size of your apple. Fold the shredded apple into the batter.

BAKE THE BLONDIES.

Pour the batter into the pan over the parchment paper. Bake for 30 to 35 minutes, until the center is no longer raw but the blondies still are a little gooey.

ADD CARAMEL AND TOPPINGS.

By themselves, these blondies remind me of a gooier apple cake. They are even more delicious served warm with a little bit of caramel sauce drizzled over the top. They are also delicious with a little bit of vanilla ice cream or even a little homemade whipped cream. (Learn how to make whipped cream on page 66.)

Changing Leaves Snickerdoodles

PREP TIME: 15 minutes | **BAKE TIME:** 11 to 13 minutes | **YIELD:** 14 to 18 cookies

In the fall, when the leaves change, it feels like the world has exploded with color. Make the colors of fall come alive in your kitchen with these yummy fall-colored snickerdoodles. You can have these cookies with a cup of apple cider after jumping in a leaf pile, but these cookies also travel well for a hike or drive to see the fall colors.

TOOLS/EQUIPMENT

- 1 or 2 baking sheets
- Parchment paper
- Cookie scoop (optional)
- Wire cooling rack or kitchen towel

½ cup (1 stick) unsalted butter, at room temperature
½ cup granulated sugar
¼ cup brown sugar
1 large egg
½ teaspoon vanilla extract
1½ teaspoons fresh lemon juice
1½ cups all-purpose flour
½ teaspoon baking soda
¼ teaspoon salt
4½ tablespoons fall-colored sugar sprinkles (red, yellow, orange)
3 teaspoons cinnamon

PREHEAT THE OVEN TO 350°F.
Line the baking sheets with parchment paper.

MIX THE WET INGREDIENTS.
In a large mixing bowl, cream together the butter, granulated sugar, and brown sugar until your batter is smooth. Add the egg, vanilla, and lemon juice, mixing all of your wet ingredients until combined.

MIX THE DRY INGREDIENTS AND MAKE A DOUGH.
In a medium mixing bowl, combine the flour, baking soda, and salt and mix. Add the dry mixture to the wet ingredients, then mix until a dough begins to form.

MIX THE COLORED CINNAMON SUGAR.
Put 1½ tablespoons of each colored sugar in a different small bowl, then add 1 teaspoon of cinnamon to each bowl and mix well. If you want some of your cookies to be brown, make one of the bowls with regular granulated sugar and cinnamon.

SCOOP THE COOKIE DOUGH.
Using a cookie scoop or a tablespoon, scoop out 2 tablespoons of dough and roll into a ball. Then roll each ball in one of the bowls of cinnamon sugar to cover the outside of the ball. Place 6 balls on each baking sheet, leaving about 2 inches between each.

Try Instead:
Some people like to press a piece of chocolate or a chocolate kiss in the middle of snickerdoodle cookies just as they come out of the oven. You can look for a fun fall flavor (caramel is good!) or a candy that is shaped like a leaf!

BAKE THE COOKIES.

Bake the cookies for 11 to 13 minutes, until gooey in the center but not raw. Allow the cookies to sit on the pan for 1 to 2 minutes, then move them to a wire rack or a clean kitchen towel to finish cooling. Enjoy!

Changing Leaves
Snickerdoodles,
page 104

Let It Snow!
Snowman Cake,
page 127

5

winter

Winter is one of the best seasons for baking! The whole season is just perfect for cozy time spent in the kitchen. Even if you don't live somewhere with cold winter weather, this is still the season that celebrates snow, classic flavors like peppermint and citrus, and lots of holidays like Christmas, Hanukkah, Valentine's Day, and even events like the Super Bowl. Get ready to make some delicious treats in this chapter—no matter the temperature outside.

Chewy Cranberry, Oatmeal, and White Chocolate Chip Cookies

PREP TIME: 20 minutes, plus 30 minutes to chill | **BAKE TIME:** 12 to 14 minutes | **YIELD:** 20 cookies

Chewy, sweet, and buttery in every bite—these cookies have it all! Make these yummy cookies for Thanksgiving in place of cranberry sauce or give them as gifts for a holly jolly Christmas cookie. Make sure to use sweetened dried cranberries or be prepared to pucker up—cranberries can be quite sour. Sweetened dried cranberries give a sweet and slightly tart flavor that goes super well with the white chocolate and the buttery dough. Yum!

TOOLS/EQUIPMENT:

- 1 or 2 baking sheets
- Parchment paper
- Electric mixer or stand mixer
- Cookie scoop (optional)

1 cup (2 sticks) unsalted butter, at room temperature

1 cup granulated sugar

½ cup brown sugar

1 large egg

2 teaspoons vanilla extract

1⅔ cups all-purpose flour

¾ teaspoon baking soda

½ teaspoon baking powder

¼ teaspoon salt

1½ cups quick oats

1 cup white chocolate chips

1 cup sweetened dried cranberries

PREHEAT THE OVEN TO 350°F.

Line the baking sheets with parchment paper.

CREAM THE BUTTER AND SUGAR AND MIX THE WET INGREDIENTS.

In a large bowl, cream together the butter, granulated sugar, and brown sugar until well mixed. Add the egg and vanilla, then continue mixing until combined.

MIX THE DRY INGREDIENTS AND MAKE A COOKIE DOUGH.

In a small mixing bowl, combine the flour, baking soda, baking powder, salt, and quick oats and mix. Add the dry mixture to the wet ingredients and mix. A dough will begin to form.

FOLD IN THE WHITE CHOCOLATE CHIPS AND CRANBERRIES.

Gently fold the white chocolate chips and the dried cranberries into your batter. Mix until everything is just combined.

CHILL THE BATTER IN THE REFRIGERATOR.

Chill your batter in the refrigerator for at least 30 minutes to keep the dough from spreading too much.

BAKE THE COOKIES.

Using a cookie scoop or a tablespoon, scoop out 2 tablespoons of dough and roll into a ball. Place 6 to 8 balls of dough on each baking sheet, leaving about 2 inches between each, and bake for 12 to 14 minutes. Don't worry if they seem a little underdone—they will keep firming up as they cool.

Sweet Orange and White Chocolate Cookies

PREP TIME: 20 minutes | **BAKE TIME:** 11 to 13 minutes | **YIELD:** 16 to 18 cookies

Heading into the winter holiday season, citrusy orange starts popping up everywhere. While the sweet flavor is in the juice inside, we can also use the orange peel to give these delicious, buttery cookies a punch of bright flavor. Then drizzle with a little white chocolate and sprinkles—yum!

TOOLS/EQUIPMENT

- 1 or 2 baking sheets
- Parchment paper
- Zester or box grater with a fine grate
- Wire cooling rack or kitchen towel

½ cup (1 stick) unsalted butter, at room temperature

½ cup sugar

½ teaspoon vanilla extract

1 orange

1½ cups all-purpose flour

¼ teaspoon salt

1 teaspoon baking soda

¾ cup white chocolate candy melts

Holiday sprinkles

PREHEAT THE OVEN TO 350°F.

Line the baking sheets with parchment paper.

START BY MIXING ALL OF THE WET INGREDIENTS.

In a large mixing bowl, cream together the butter and sugar until well mixed. Next add the vanilla to your dough and mix well.

ZEST AND JUICE THE ORANGE.

Rinse the orange and dry it with a towel. Using the smallest holes on a box grater (or a zester), gently zest the peel of the orange. Zest only the orange skin, not the white underneath. Cut the orange in half and squeeze the juice from both halves into a small bowl. You should have about ¼ cup of freshly squeezed orange juice and 1 teaspoon of zest. Add the juice and zest to your wet ingredients.

MIX IN THE DRY INGREDIENTS.

In a second bowl, add the flour, salt, and baking soda. Mix well, then add the dry ingredients to the wet ingredients and mix until a dough forms.

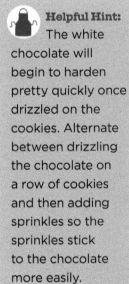

Helpful Hint: The white chocolate will begin to harden pretty quickly once drizzled on the cookies. Alternate between drizzling the chocolate on a row of cookies and then adding sprinkles so the sprinkles stick to the chocolate more easily.

ROLL THE COOKIE DOUGH AND BAKE THE COOKIES.
Roll your cookie dough into dough balls that are about the size of a ping-pong ball, about 1 inch each. Place 6 dough balls on each baking sheet, leaving space between the cookies for them to spread as they cook, and bake for 11 to 13 minutes.

DRIZZLE WITH WHITE CHOCOLATE AND SPRINKLES.
Melt the white chocolate candy melts in a small bowl according to the directions on the package. With the cookies on a piece of parchment paper, drizzle melted white chocolate over your cookies (milk and dark chocolate work, too). Add sprinkles right away, before the chocolate becomes firm.

Stained Glass
Cookie Ornaments,
page 115

Stained Glass Cookie Ornaments

PREP TIME: 45 minutes | **BAKE TIME:** 10 to 13 minutes | **YIELD:** 14 to 17 cookies

Stained glass cookies start as sugar cookies but look so much like colorful Christmas ornaments that you'll want to hang them on the tree. This version uses fruity, chewy gummies that look simply beautiful once melted. Use all of a single-color gummy or mix the colored gummy pieces for a rainbow swirl look. Store these cookies in a sealed container so the gummies stay soft in the center.

TOOLS/EQUIPMENT

- 2 baking sheets
- Parchment paper
- Electric mixer or stand mixer (optional)
- Whisk (optional)
- Rolling pin
- 2 chopsticks (optional)
- 3-inch round cookie cutter
- 1½- to 2-inch cookie cutters in holiday shapes
- Toothpick

¾ cup (1½ sticks) unsalted butter, cold

¾ cup sugar

2 large eggs

½ teaspoon vanilla extract

2¼ cups all-purpose flour, plus more for dusting the work surface

½ teaspoon salt

8 ounces gummy bears (gummy worms work, too!)

PREHEAT THE OVEN TO 350°F.

Line the baking sheets with parchment paper.

MIX THE WET INGREDIENTS.

In a large mixing bowl with a strong wooden spoon or electric mixer or in the bowl of a stand mixer, cream the butter and sugar together for 2 to 3 minutes on medium-low speed. Next, separate an egg by cracking it open over two bowls and allowing the egg white to drip into a bowl while holding the yolk in the shell. Drop the yolk into a second bowl. In the bowl with the yolk, crack and add a second full egg and the vanilla, then beat with a fork or whisk. Add the egg mixture to your sugar and butter and mix until well blended. (You can discard the extra egg white from the first egg, or save for another recipe, like the Gooey Passover Double-Chocolate Flourless Cookies on page 36).

MIX THE COOKIE DOUGH.

To your wet mixture, add the flour and scatter the salt around the bowl. Mix well for a few minutes with a wooden spoon or a stand mixer on low until a dough

❯ CONTINUED

forms. (Don't try mixing this part of the dough with an electric hand mixer—the dough is very thick and may break your mixer!)

ROLL OUT THE COOKIE DOUGH.

Lightly flour a clean counter and the rolling pin. Roll out your dough, adding flour to the top of it. Lay two chopsticks on either side of your dough. Roll until it is about ⅜ inch thick, a little thicker than a chopstick. Use a 3-inch cookie cutter and cut circles out of your dough.

CUT THE DOUGH WITH COOKIE CUTTERS.

In the center of each circle, use a small holiday cookie cutter that is 1½ to 2 inches to cut the center out of each cookie. Take a small piece of dough about the size of a large bean and roll it into a ball, then flatten it and press it at the top of your circle for the Christmas tree ornament.

BAKE THE COOKIES (BUT NOT ALL THE WAY THROUGH).

Reroll any extra dough to cut more cookies. Bake the cookies for 9 to 11 minutes until they are almost done. Don't worry, they will cook more in the next step.

MELT GUMMY CANDY IN THE CENTERS.

Slice your gummy candies into the smallest pieces you can. First slice longways to make them thinner, and then into pieces just a little bigger than a sprinkle. While the cookies are still hot on the pan, sprinkle the gummy bits into the center of the cookies. You can use one color in each center or mix them! Put the cookies back in the oven for 1 to 2 minutes to melt the gummies.

COOL THE COOKIES TO SET.

Use a toothpick to pull the gummy candy to fill in any holes while the cookies are still warm. Once the pan has cooled for a few minutes, put the baking sheet in the refrigerator for about 5 minutes to fully set the gummies.

Helpful Hint: If you don't have a tiny cookie cutter, you can also use an icing decorating tip to cut polka dots from your ornaments. Making the cookies like this will result in fewer cookies, but they are still delicious—and fun!

Chocolate Chip and Almond Spanish Polvorones

PREP TIME: 30 minutes | **BAKE TIME:** 10 to 12 minutes | **YIELD:** 16 to 19 cookies

Polvorones, Russian tea cakes, snowballs, Mexican wedding cookies—these cookies have so many names! They are a Spanish Christmas treat, but they definitely make their way onto cookie trays all around the world at the holidays. Whatever name you use, these shortbread cookies use butter to hold them together and are double-rolled in powdered sugar. Let these cookies cool completely before storing them so the powdered sugar doesn't melt off.

TOOLS/EQUIPMENT

- 2 baking sheets
- Parchment paper
- Cutting board

½ cup (1 stick) unsalted butter, at room temperature

¼ cup powdered sugar, plus 1 cup for rolling

½ teaspoon vanilla extract

¼ teaspoon almond extract

1 cup all-purpose flour

¼ teaspoon salt

½ cup sliced almonds or walnut or pecan pieces

¼ cup mini chocolate chips

PREHEAT THE OVEN TO 350°F.

Line the baking sheets with parchment paper.

CREAM THE BUTTER AND SUGAR.

In a large mixing bowl, cream the butter and ¼ cup of powdered sugar together until well combined. Add the vanilla and almond extract, then mix well.

MIX THE DRY INGREDIENTS AND MAKE A DOUGH.

Add the flour and salt to the wet ingredients. Take extra care with the salt to sprinkle it around the bowl and not all in one spot. Mix well.

CHOP THE NUTS.

On a cutting board, chop up the nuts evenly. If using regular-size chocolate chips (not mini), chop your chocolate a little bit, just as you've done with the nuts. Fold the nuts and chocolate into the batter and chill the batter for 15 minutes in the refrigerator.

ROLL AND BAKE THE COOKIES.

Using a tablespoon, measure and roll balls of dough and place 8 balls on each baking sheet. Cook for 10 to 12 minutes, until just slightly brown on the bottom when you lift the cookie up with a spatula. Let your cookies cool for 1 to 2 minutes and then move them quickly to a plate.

Trouble-shooting: It is so tempting to roll these cookies right away, but if you roll the second layer of powdered sugar too soon, it will melt onto your cookie and the cookie won't be fluffy. Also wait until your cookies have cooled completely to store them, or they may get soggy!

ROLL YOUR COOKIES IN POWDERED SUGAR—TWICE.

Put 1 cup of powdered sugar in a small bowl. Roll each cookie in powdered sugar and place back on the plate. The heat from the first layer of powdered sugar will melt the sugar a little, but the first layer of powdered sugar won't stick unless you add it while the cookies are warm. Once the cookies have cooled all the way, roll the cookies in powdered sugar a second time to give them the fluffy snowball look. Enjoy!

The Biggest Cinnamon-Sugar Christmas Donut Ever

PREP TIME: 20 minutes | **BAKE TIME:** 30 to 40 minutes | **YIELD:** 12 slices

What's more fun than a holiday donut? A GIANT donut! This giant donut has a surprise cinnamon-sugar swirl inside from stacking individual mini donut holes in the pan. I learned this technique from my husband's mother when she taught me to make monkey bread. This donut is perfect for sharing with your family and friends for breakfast, brunch, or dessert. You can also swap the colors for other holidays. It's delicious for an Easter brunch, too.

TOOLS/EQUIPMENT

- Silicone brush
- 10-inch Bundt pan
- Plastic cling wrap
- Stand mixer (optional)
- Baking sheet
- Toothpick
- 3 sandwich bags or piping bags

1 cup (2 sticks) plus
    1 tablespoon butter
    at room temperature,
    divided
4¼ cups all-purpose
    flour, divided
1¼ cups buttermilk
4 teaspoons
    baking powder
1 teaspoon baking soda
¾ cup granulated sugar
3 tablespoons cinnamon
2 cups powdered sugar
¼ cup milk
½ cup red candy melts
½ cup green candy melts
Sprinkles

PREHEAT THE OVEN TO 350°F.

Melt 1 tablespoon of butter and use a silicone brush to coat the entire inside of the Bundt pan. Some newer Bundt pans meant for lighter cakes like angel food cake are two pieces, but this cake needs a one-piece pan so the butter doesn't drip out.

FLOUR THE PAN.

Add ¼ cup of flour to the Bundt pan and cover tightly with a piece of cling wrap. Gently tip the pan around until the flour coats every surface evenly, then tap out any extra flour and discard the cling wrap.

MIX THE DOUGH.

In a large mixing bowl with a strong wooden spoon or in the bowl of a stand mixer, mix the buttermilk and ¾ cup of room-temperature butter until combined. In another large mixing bowl, combine the remaining 4 cups of flour, the baking powder, and baking soda. Add the flour mixture to the wet ingredients slowly, 1 to 2 cups at a time, on low speed until a dough ball forms.

ROLL THE DOUGH.

Melt the remaining ¼ cup of butter in a small bowl. In a second small bowl, mix the granulated sugar with cinnamon. Roll the dough into 1-inch balls, slightly smaller than a ping-pong ball. Roll each dough ball in the melted butter, then the cinnamon sugar, and place in the pan. Fill the pan about three-quarters full with dough balls, then place the Bundt pan on a baking sheet to move it in and out of the oven easily.

BAKE THE GIANT DONUT.

Bake the donut for 30 to 40 minutes, until a toothpick inserted in the center comes out clean. Allow the donut to cool in the pan for several minutes, then flip onto a platter to finish cooling. The donut may have a few cracks because it is dough balls, not solid cake. Gently push the donut together before it cools.

FROST AND DECORATE THE DONUT.

Mix together the powdered sugar and milk. Place the mixture in a plastic sandwich bag and snip a tiny piece off the corner. Drizzle glaze back and forth across the donut, working in a circle. Melt the candy melts according to the package directions and fill the sandwich bags. Drizzle the candy melts over the cake and top with sprinkles.

Christmas Cutout Cookies

PREP TIME: 45 minutes | **BAKE TIME:** 9 to 11 minutes | **YIELD:** 14 to 17 cookies

Baking cutout cookies and decorating them with icing is a widespread tradition, and many families make sure to try it every year. This recipe uses a royal icing made with meringue powder, that you dip and decorate, but you can also use the buttercream frosting on page 52. This technique can create simple, fancy, or supercute cookies, so let your imagination run wild.

TOOLS/EQUIPMENT

- 2 baking sheets
- Parchment paper
- Stand mixer (optional)
- Whisk (optional)
- Rolling pin
- 2 chopsticks (optional)
- Holiday cookie cutters
- Piping bags or strong plastic zip-top bags

FOR THE COOKIES

1 cup (2 sticks) unsalted butter, cold
1 cup granulated sugar
2 large eggs, cold
½ teaspoon vanilla extract
3 cups all-purpose flour, plus more for dusting
½ teaspoon salt

FOR THE BASE ICING

2 cups powdered sugar
¼ cup water
2 tablespoons meringue powder
1 teaspoon vanilla extract

PREHEAT THE OVEN TO 350°F.

Line the baking sheets with parchment paper.

MIX THE WET INGREDIENTS.

In a large mixing bowl with a strong wooden spoon or in the bowl of a stand mixer, cream the butter and granulated sugar together. In a small bowl, crack the eggs and beat with a fork or whisk. Add the eggs and vanilla to the butter-sugar mixture, then mix until well blended.

ADD THE DRY INGREDIENTS.

To your wet mixture, add the flour and scatter the salt around the bowl. Mix well for a few minutes with a wooden spoon or a stand mixer on low speed until a dough forms. (Don't try mixing this part of the dough with an electric hand mixer—the dough is very thick and may break your mixer!)

ROLL OUT THE COOKIE DOUGH.

Lightly flour a clean counter and the rolling pin. Roll out your dough, adding flour to the top of your dough. Lay two chopsticks on either side of your dough. Roll until it is about ⅜ inch thick, a little thicker than a chopstick.

CUT THE DOUGH WITH COOKIE CUTTERS.

Use your holiday cookie cutters and cut out your favorite holiday shapes. Santa, reindeer, stars, trees—use your favorite shapes to make cute cookies!

FOR EACH DECORATIVE ICING COLOR

1 cup powdered sugar
2 tablespoons water
1 tablespoon meringue powder
½ teaspoon vanilla extract
Food coloring assortment (gel food coloring makes brighter colors)

 Helpful Hint: Sometimes the colors from the decorating icing can bleed into the base color. Letting your cookies fully chill and set helps, so don't pull them out of the refrigerator too fast. If you live in a humid area, you may need to leave them in the refrigerator longer.

BAKE THE COOKIES.

Reroll any extra dough to cut more cookies. Bake your cookies in the oven for 9 to 11 minutes. Try to put similar-size cookies all on the same pan. If you put tiny cookies with large cookies, you are more likely to overcook the small cookies or underbake the large cookies. Cool your cookies completely before you start icing, or the icing will melt off the cookies.

DIP THE COOKIES IN ICING.

Make the base color icing by mixing together 2 cups of powdered sugar, ¼ cup of water, 2 tablespoons of meringue powder, and 1 teaspoon of vanilla. Your base color can be white, but don't be afraid to change it to red, green, or even brown depending on your shapes. Dip the top of each cookie in the icing, then chill cookies in the refrigerator for at least 15 to 20 minutes.

DECORATE DETAILS WITH ICING.

Mix up each color of icing by mixing together 1 cup of powdered sugar, 2 tablespoons of water, 1 tablespoon of meringue powder, ½ teaspoon of vanilla, and gel food coloring. Add the icing to a piping bag as explained on page 19. Use your icing to draw, dot, and decorate the cookies. Place the decorated cookies in the refrigerator for 5 to 10 minutes to set the icing.

Chocolate-Peppermint
Crinkle Cookies,
page 125

Chocolate-Peppermint Crinkle Cookies

PREP TIME: 45 minutes | **BAKE TIME:** 12 to 14 minutes | **YIELD:** 16 to 17 cookies

Chocolate-Peppermint Crinkle Cookies are irresistible, with their cloudlike outside and fudgy center. The original crinkle cookie was a molasses cookie, but these days chocolate crinkle cookies rule. Surprise your friends and family by adding a peppermint twist! These cookies bake up puffy and look impressive with the dark chocolate peeking out from behind the snowy powdered sugar.

TOOLS/EQUIPMENT
- 2 baking sheets
- Parchment paper
- Whisk (optional)
- Wire cooling rack or kitchen towel

---

4 tablespoons (½ stick) unsalted butter, at room temperature

½ cup granulated sugar

1 cold large egg, beaten

2 tablespoons yogurt

½ teaspoon peppermint extract

¼ teaspoon vanilla extract

1 cup all-purpose flour

⅓ cup unsweetened cocoa powder

1 teaspoon baking powder

¼ teaspoon salt

¾ cup powdered sugar

PREHEAT THE OVEN TO 350°F.

Line the baking sheets with parchment paper.

CREAM AND MIX THE WET INGREDIENTS.

In a large mixing bowl with a strong wooden spoon, cream the butter and granulated sugar together in a mashing motion until there is no more loose sugar. Next crack and beat the egg in a small bowl with a fork or whisk and add it to the butter-sugar mixture. Add the yogurt, peppermint extract, and vanilla and mix until well combined. The dough will be thick.

MIX THE DRY INGREDIENTS, THEN CHILL.

In a medium bowl, add the flour, cocoa, baking powder, and salt and mix until well combined. Add your dry ingredients to your wet ingredients and mix well until you have a thick, fudgy dough. Place your bowl of dough in the refrigerator for 10 to 15 minutes to chill.

› CONTINUED

Try Instead: If you would rather skip the minty twist, substitute extra vanilla for the peppermint extract. You can also press a chocolate or chocolate-peppermint candy into the center of each of these cookies while they are still hot to make a kiss cookie!

ROLL THE COOKIES IN POWDERED SUGAR AND CHILL AGAIN.

Roll the dough into 1-inch cookie balls a little bigger than an extra-large grape and place all of them on a piece of parchment paper on one baking sheet. Try to make the cookies even in size. Roll each of the dough balls in a bowl of powdered sugar. Place the entire sheet full of cookie dough balls back in the refrigerator for about 5 minutes.

ROLL THE COOKIES IN POWDERED SUGAR—AGAIN!

Roll all of the cookie dough balls in powdered sugar again, covering the entire dough ball. This time arrange them on parchment paper on two baking sheets, about 8 balls to each pan. Don't skip this second rolling—this is what gives these cookies the crinkle and snow-ball look.

BAKE THE COOKIES.

Bake the cookies in the oven for 12 to 14 minutes. Your cookies should puff up, and dark crinkles will start to show as they bake. Your cookies will still be slightly fudgy in the middle but not raw inside. Leave the cookies to cool for a few minutes on a pan, then transfer to a wire rack or towel. Enjoy every bite!

Let It Snow! Snowman Cake

PREP TIME: 50 minutes, plus 2 hours to chill | **BAKE TIME:** 30 to 35 minutes | **YIELD:** 12 slices

Let it snow with this super-fun cake! This snowman is a larger dessert, perfect to share. Freezing the cake for at least 2 hours before you add frosting is an important step so the cake doesn't crumble. You can also freeze it overnight. This *is* a snowman, after all! Use any extra frosting to add details like earmuffs, a snowflake, or eyelashes!

TOOLS/EQUIPMENT

- Pencil
- 9-inch round cake pan
- Parchment paper
- Clean kitchen scissors
- Toothpick
- Electric mixer or stand mixer
- Piping bag or strong plastic zip-top bag

FOR THE CAKE

Oil, for greasing the pan
2 large eggs
¾ cup granulated sugar
½ cup yogurt
½ cup oil
2 teaspoons vanilla extract
1¼ cups all-purpose flour
1½ teaspoons baking powder
½ teaspoon baking soda
½ teaspoon salt

PREHEAT THE OVEN TO 350°F.

With a pencil, trace your cake pan on a piece of parchment paper, cut out the circle with clean kitchen scissors, and place it in the bottom of the cake pan. Then lightly oil the sides of the pan so the cake won't stick.

MIX THE CAKE BATTER.

In a large mixing bowl, beat the eggs. Add the granulated sugar, yogurt, oil, and 2 teaspoons of vanilla and mix well until combined. In a medium mixing bowl, combine the flour, baking powder, baking soda, and salt and mix well. Add your dry mixture to your wet ingredients and mix well.

PREPARE THE CAKE PAN AND BAKE YOUR CAKE.

Pour the cake batter in the pan and bake the cake for 30 to 35 minutes, until a toothpick inserted in the center comes out clean, then let the cake cool.

FREEZE THE CAKE UNTIL FIRM.

Once your cake has cooled, place it in the freezer for at least 2 hours.

› CONTINUED

FOR THE FROSTING AND DECORATIONS

1 cup (2 sticks) unsalted butter, at room temperature
8 ounces cream cheese, at room temperature
4 cups powdered sugar
2 teaspoons vanilla extract
Orange food coloring
Chocolate candies (like M&M's)

MAKE THE CREAM CHEESE FROSTING.

Once the cake is frozen, make the frosting. In a large mixing bowl with an electric mixer or in the bowl of a stand mixer, whip the butter for 5 minutes. Scrape down the sides of the bowl and add the cream cheese, then beat for 1 to 2 minutes more. Scrape down the bowl and add the powdered sugar ½ cup at a time. Once mixed, add 2 teaspoons of vanilla and mix for 1 minute more. Remove ½ cup of frosting and set aside in a small bowl for the snowman nose.

ADD A CRUMB COAT TO YOUR CAKE.

On your cake plate, place a dollop of frosting (this will help the cake stay still), then add your cake. Frost a thin layer of icing over your cake top and sides to hold in the crumbs (this is called a crumb coat). You will still see the cake through the icing, and some crumbly bits may come off—this is OK! Place the cake in the refrigerator for 10 minutes.

FROST THE SNOWMAN CAKE.

Starting at the top of your cake, add a thicker layer of frosting. Work from the center of the cake, spreading the icing toward the outside of the top. Then add a dollop of frosting to the edge of the cake and work it down the side of the cake. Keep working your way around the cake, adding dollops of icing and pulling them down until you have a thick layer of icing. Use your metal spatula to smooth out the icing.

Color your small bowl of icing orange with food coloring and place it in a piping bag or zip-top bag. (See instructions for filling a piping bag on page 19.) Use your chocolate candies to make eyes, a smile, and even rosy cheeks. Use your orange icing to draw a carrot nose on your cake.

Did You Know? The world's tallest snowman was actually a snowwoman—she was built in Maine, using trees for arms!

Chocolate-Cinnamon Rugelach Cookies

PREP TIME: 20 minutes | **BAKE TIME:** 13 to 15 minutes | **YIELD:** 12 cookies

This tasty dessert is often served for Hanukkah (and even Shavuot, which is shortly after Passover) and is a crowd favorite! The name *rugelach* means "little twists" for the crescent shape of the cookies. The most popular cookies are filled with chocolate, but sometimes you'll find them full of apricot jam, gooey cinnamon sugar, or even nuts. This version has a combination of chocolate with a tiny bit of cinnamon to make them extra warm and cozy.

TOOLS/EQUIPMENT

- 1 or 2 baking sheets
- Parchment paper
- Rolling pin
- Cutting board
- Silicone brush

1½ cups self-rising flour, plus more for rolling

¾ cup vanilla Greek yogurt

2 tablespoons unsalted butter, melted, divided

¼ cup sugar, plus more for sprinkling

1 teaspoon cinnamon

½ cup mini chocolate chips or chopped chocolate

PREHEAT YOUR OVEN TO 375°F.

Line the baking sheets with parchment paper.

MIX THE DOUGH.

In a large mixing bowl, mix together the self-rising flour (see page 9 for more details about this special flour) and Greek yogurt with a silicone spatula until a dough forms. Add a handful of flour to your clean kitchen counter to keep your dough from sticking. Place the dough ball on top of your floured surface and knead the dough with your hands for 1 to 2 minutes. Flip and stretch the dough until it stretches easily like a pizza dough.

ROLL THE DOUGH INTO A CIRCLE AND SLICE INTO PIECES.

Dust your rolling pin with flour and sprinkle more flour on your counter. Roll the dough into a thin sheet, working it from the center into a circle shape that is about 10 inches across and around ¼ inch thick. When the dough is big enough, move it to a floured cutting board. Flip your mixing bowl over the dough and trace it with a butter knife to make your dough a circle. Slice your dough into 12 even pieces like you are cutting a pizza.

FILL THE COOKIES WITH GOOEY FILLING.

Take the silicone brush and 1 tablespoon of melted butter and brush butter all over your dough. In a small bowl, mix the sugar and cinnamon and sprinkle on your dough evenly. Sprinkle your mini chocolate chips all over your dough. It is helpful for rolling to put more of the chocolate toward the outside of the circle, but make sure to put some in the middle, too.

ROLL THE COOKIES.

Starting at the wider end, roll each triangle of dough toward the point. Place each rolled cookie on the baking sheet with the triangle points down so they don't unroll. A little bit of the filling will spill as you roll—that's OK, just scoop what you can back into the cookies as you roll.

BAKE THE COOKIES.

Pinch the ends of your cookies and bend them a little so they are a horn shape. Brush the tops of the cookies with the remaining 1 tablespoon of melted butter and sprinkle with a little extra sugar if you want to. Then bake the cookies for 13 to 15 minutes until gooey and delicious.

Super Bowl Football Field Cookie Bars

PREP TIME: 45 minutes | **BAKE TIME:** 45 to 50 minutes | **YIELD:** 24

One of the most popular sporting events of the year, the Super Bowl is also one of the most popular events for snacking! While many of us chow down on savory foods like pizza and guacamole, what party table is complete without the perfect dessert? These football field cookie bars will outshine the halftime show—serve them straight out of the pan and don't forget to customize with this year's Super Bowl number across the top!

TOOLS/EQUIPMENT

- Pencil
- 8-by-11-inch baking pan
- Parchment paper
- Clean kitchen scissors
- Electric mixer or stand mixer
- Piping bag or strong plastic zip-top bag
- Chopstick (optional)

FOR THE COOKIE BARS

1 cup (2 sticks) unsalted butter, at room temperature
1 cup brown sugar
½ cup granulated sugar
2 large eggs
1 teaspoon vanilla extract
3 cups all-purpose flour
1 teaspoon baking soda
½ teaspoon salt
1½ cups chocolate candies (like M&M's), plus more for decorating

PREHEAT THE OVEN TO 350°F.
With a pencil, trace your pan on a piece of parchment paper, cut out the rectangle with clean kitchen scissors, and place it in the bottom of the pan.

MIX TOGETHER THE WET INGREDIENTS.
In a large mixing bowl, cream together 1 cup of butter, brown sugar, and granulated sugar until smooth without lumps of butter. Add the eggs and 1 teaspoon of vanilla and mix well until combined.

MIX THE DRY INGREDIENTS TOGETHER TO MAKE THE COOKIE DOUGH.
In a medium mixing bowl, combine the flour, baking soda, and salt. Add the flour mixture to your wet ingredients, then mix until it makes a smooth and thick dough. Fold the chocolate candies into the dough.

BAKE THE COOKIE BARS UNTIL THEY ARE GOOEY.
Scoop the cookie dough into the pan. Use clean hands to press the dough in evenly. Bake the cookie bars for 45 to 50 minutes, until puffy and just cooked all the way through. Let the cookie bars cool all the way before frosting.

Super Bowl Football
Field Cookie Bars,
page 132

FOR THE FROSTING

½ cup (1 stick) unsalted butter, at room temperature

4 ounces cream cheese (half a block), at room temperature

2 cups powdered sugar

1 teaspoon vanilla extract

Green food coloring

MAKE THE CREAM CHEESE FROSTING.

In a large mixing bowl with an electric mixer, or in the bowl of a stand mixer, beat ½ cup of butter for 5 minutes, watching it turn a slightly lighter color. Scrape down the sides of the bowl and add the cream cheese, beating it for 1 to 2 minutes. Scrape down your bowl again and add the powdered sugar slowly, ½ cup at a time. Add 1 teaspoon of vanilla and beat for 1 minute more. Place ½ cup white frosting into a piping bag. (See instructions for loading a piping bag on page 19.)

DECORATE THE FOOTBALL FIELD COOKIE BARS WITH FROSTING.

Add green food coloring to the large bowl of frosting a little at a time and mix until green. Frost the entire pan of cookie bars with the green frosting as evenly as you can. With the white frosting, draw a 50-yard line down the middle of the field and draw 3 more yard lines evenly on each side of the 50 down the pan. (You can have someone hold a chopstick over the cookie pan, then draw your field lines along the chopstick for a straighter yard line.) Then add chocolate candies for the players. Enjoy!

> **Helpful Hint:** You don't have to draw every single yard line found on a regular football field—just draw a few and write numbers on a few of the yard lines (like the 50 and the 30) to give the idea of a football field.

Lunar New Year Walnut Cookies

PREP TIME: 30 minutes | **BAKE TIME:** 10 to 12 minutes | **YIELD:** 16 to 17 cookies

Lunar New Year, also sometimes called Chinese New Year, celebrates the end of winter—though it's often still quite chilly out when it rolls around in January or February. Traditional sweets include rice pudding, candied fruit, crispy dumplings, and walnut cookies. Sweets are very important to this holiday because they are said to sweeten up the coming year. The holiday itself lasts for 15 days, so you have plenty of time to celebrate! These walnut cookies are sweet, nutty, and just a little crumbly in the best way.

TOOLS/EQUIPMENT

- 2 baking sheets
- Parchment paper
- Whisk (optional)
- Cutting board (optional)
- Food processor (optional)

½ cup (1 stick) unsalted butter, at room temperature
½ cup brown sugar
¼ cup granulated sugar
2 large eggs
½ teaspoon vanilla extract
2 cups all-purpose flour
1 teaspoon baking powder
½ teaspoon baking soda
½ teaspoon salt
½ cup chopped walnuts, plus more for decorating

PREHEAT THE OVEN TO 350°F.
Line the baking sheets with parchment paper.

CREAM TOGETHER THE BUTTER AND SUGAR.
In a large mixing bowl, cream the butter, brown sugar, and granulated sugar together until combined. In a small bowl, crack the eggs and beat them with a fork or whisk to break the yolks. Add the eggs and vanilla to your butter-sugar mixture and mix until smooth.

MIX THE DRY INGREDIENTS AND MAKE A DOUGH.
In a medium mixing bowl, add the flour, baking powder, baking soda, and salt. Mix until well combined. Add the dry ingredients to your wet ingredients to make a dough.

CHOP AND FOLD IN THE WALNUTS.
Set aside some larger walnuts for decorating your cookies—you'll want 16 larger pieces. Place the rest of the walnuts on a cutting board and chop them up. The nuts should be smaller than a quarter of a walnut, but not turned into dust. You can also use a food processor to chop the nuts with the pulse button. But be careful—if the walnuts are blended too long, they will turn into walnut butter. Once you have the walnuts chopped, fold them into the dough.

> CONTINUED

Did You Know?

Walnuts mean happiness for Lunar New Year, and everyone wants happiness for the coming year. Make a plate of happiness for your family and celebrate a fresh beginning to the year.

DIVIDE THE DOUGH INTO EVEN BALLS.

Roll the dough into a giant ball, then divide the dough in half. Now divide each of those dough balls in half. Use your 4 dough balls to make 4 cookies each and place your cookies on the prepared baking sheets.

PRESS THE COOKIES JUST A LITTLE, DECORATE WITH WALNUTS, AND BAKE!

With the back of a fork, press down on your dough ball, flattening the cookies, then turn the fork and press down again the other direction. You're creating a tic-tac-toe board on the cookies. Place a larger walnut piece on one side of each cookie. Now bake the cookies for 10 to 12 minutes, until slightly crumbly and brown on the bottom.

Raspberry Sweetheart Rolls

PREP TIME: 20 minutes | **BAKE TIME:** 10 to 12 minutes | **YIELD:** 12 rolls

Tell someone just how much you love them for Valentine's Day and make these raspberry heart-shaped rolls. These gooey sweet rolls are packed full of sweet raspberry flavor and are perfect for a yummy treat—or maybe even breakfast. Jam or fruit preserves work best in this recipe, as both are made with sweetened whole fruit. (Jelly is made from sweetened fruit juice and won't be as flavorful.) Try cutting your dough in half when you roll it out and making two different flavors!

TOOLS/EQUIPMENT
- 1 or 2 baking sheets
- Parchment paper
- Rolling pin

1½ cups self-rising flour, plus more for dusting the work surface
¾ cup vanilla Greek yogurt
6 tablespoons raspberry jam or preserves
½ cup powdered sugar
4 teaspoons milk

PREHEAT YOUR OVEN TO 375°F.
Line the baking sheets with parchment paper.

MIX THE DOUGH FOR THE ROLLS.
In a large bowl with a silicone spatula, mix together the self-rising flour (see page 9 for more details about this special flour) and Greek yogurt until combined. Add a handful of flour to a clean kitchen counter. Place the dough ball on the counter, kneading with your hands for 1 to 2 minutes. Flip and stretch the dough until it stretches easily like a pizza dough.

ROLL THE DOUGH FLAT.
Using a rolling pin, roll the dough into a thin sheet. Work the dough from the center, stretching it a little at a time with your rolling pin. Roll the dough into a rectangle shape. Your dough rectangle should be about 12 inches wide by 10 inches tall.

FILL YOUR DOUGH AND ROLL INTO A HEART SHAPE.
Spoon the jam onto the dough and spread a thin layer over the entire dough. From the bottom of the dough, begin rolling tightly until you reach halfway up your dough. From the top, roll the dough tightly down until you reach the middle and the first roll.

> CONTINUED

Trouble-shooting: If a hole forms while you are rolling the dough with a rolling pin, pinch your dough back together and roll over that spot again! Try to keep your dough the same thickness across the entire sheet.

SLICE AND BAKE THE HEART ROLLS.

Using a sharp knife, cut the dough in half. Cut each half evenly into 6 pieces. Place 6 heart rolls on your baking sheet with at least 2 inches between each. Pinch the bottom of each heart to form a point. Bake each batch for 10 to 12 minutes.

MAKE AND DRIZZLE THE GLAZE.

In a small bowl, use a spoon to combine the powdered sugar with the milk. Mix the sugar well until a gooey glaze forms. Drizzle the glaze over the warm rolls just after they finish baking.

Raspberry Sweetheart
Rolls, page 137

"Whoopie! Thanks for
Being My Teacher" Pies,
page 146

6

all year round

A big holiday on the calendar might be the perfect reason to make a special treat—but some celebrations happen all year long! Here you'll find plenty of ideas to celebrate birthdays and anniversaries, delicious ways to say thanks, treats to bring to a bake sale, and even a special treat to share with your favorite puppy!

141

Choco-Vanilla
Birthday Cake,
page 143

Choco-Vanilla Birthday Cake

PREP TIME: 75 minutes, plus 2 hours to chill | **BAKE TIME:** 30 to 35 minutes | **YIELD:** 12 slices

Happy birthday! Celebrate with this yummy layered cake topped with frosting and plenty of sprinkles. Sometimes for a birthday, it can be hard to decide what flavor of cake to make. This cake gives you a dose of both chocolate and vanilla, so you don't have to choose. You could also use this recipe to make an all-chocolate or all-vanilla cake. You can thank the ancient Greeks and Romans for this, as the tradition of having a cake for a birthday goes all the way back to them!

TOOLS/EQUIPMENT

- Pencil
- 2 (9-inch) round cake pans
- Parchment paper
- Toothpick
- Electric mixer or stand mixer
- Cookie cutter (any shape)

FOR THE CHOCOLATE LAYER

½ cup oil, plus more for greasing the pans

2 large eggs

¾ cup granulated sugar

½ cup yogurt

2 teaspoons vanilla extract

1 cup all-purpose flour

½ cup unsweetened cocoa powder

1½ teaspoons baking powder

½ teaspoon baking soda

½ teaspoon salt

PREHEAT THE OVEN TO 350°F.

With a pencil, trace your cake pans on parchment paper, cut out the circles with clean kitchen scissors, and place them in the bottom of the cake pans. Lightly oil the sides of the pan.

MIX THE BATTERS.

To make the chocolate layer, in a large mixing bowl, beat the eggs. Add the granulated sugar, yogurt, ½ cup of oil, and 2 teaspoons of vanilla and mix well until combined. In a medium mixing bowl, combine the flour, cocoa, baking powder, baking soda, and salt. Mix until well combined. Add your flour mixture to your wet ingredients and mix the batter well. Repeat this step with the ingredients for the vanilla cake layer.

BAKE THE CAKES.

Pour each cake batter into a pan and bake the cakes for 30 to 35 minutes, until a toothpick inserted in the center comes out clean. Then let the cakes cool.

› CONTINUED

FOR THE VANILLA LAYER

2 large eggs
¾ cup granulated sugar
½ cup yogurt
½ cup oil
2 teaspoons
    vanilla extract
1¼ cups all-purpose flour
1½ teaspoons
    baking powder
½ teaspoon baking soda
½ teaspoon salt

FOR THE CREAM CHEESE FROSTING

1½ cups (3 sticks)
    unsalted butter, at
    room temperature
12 ounces cream cheese,
    at room temperature
6 cups powdered sugar
1 tablespoon
    vanilla extract
Sprinkles

FREEZE THE CAKES UNTIL FIRM.

Once your cakes are cool, place them in the freezer. Freezing the cake is important so your cake doesn't crumble when you add icing. Leave your cake in the freezer for at least 2 hours, but you can also freeze them overnight in a container, which makes it much easier to frost.

MAKE THE CREAM CHEESE FROSTING.

In a large mixing bowl with an electric mixer or in the bowl of a stand mixer, whip your butter for 5 minutes. Scrape down the sides of the bowl, add the cream cheese, and beat for 1 to 2 minutes more. Scrape down the sides of the bowl and add the powdered sugar to your mixture ½ cup at a time, mixing well between each addition. Add 1 tablespoon of vanilla and mix for 1 minute more.

LAYER THE CAKE.

On the cake plate, place a dollop of frosting so your cake stays still, then add the first cake to the cake plate. Now add 1 cup of frosting and spread evenly over the top of the cake for the filling in between the layers. Add the top layer of the cake upside down to give your cake a nice flat top to frost.

ADD A CRUMB COAT OF FROSTING.

Frost a thin layer of icing over your cake top and sides to hold in the crumbs (this is called a crumb coat). You will still see the cake through the icing—this is OK! Place the cake in the refrigerator for 10 minutes to help set the icing.

Trouble-shooting: If you find yourself having a hard time getting the frosting even, try putting your cake in the refrigerator for 5 to 10 minutes. This sets the icing just a little and makes it easier to make smooth. Putting your cake in the refrigerator or freezer for a little longer can also help if your cake starts pulling crumbs while you are frosting.

FROST THE CAKE.

Starting at the top of your cake, add a thicker layer of frosting to your cake. Work from the center of the cake, spreading the icing toward the outside of the cake. Then add a dollop of frosting to the edge and work it down the side of the cake. Keep working your way around the cake until you have a thick layer of frosting on your cake. Use your metal spatula to smooth out the cake as needed. If you find your cake is pulling or crumbing, it's OK! Try putting your cake back in the refrigerator for a little while (at least 15 minutes), then try again.

ADD SPRINKLES.

Place your favorite-shaped cookie cutter on your cake, then carefully add sprinkles to the outside of the cookie cutter only. When you remove the cookie cutter, the shape will still be on your cake in icing! You can also color any extra frosting with food coloring and write "Happy Birthday" on the cake.

"Whoopie! Thanks for Being My Teacher" Pies

PREP TIME: 45 minutes | **BAKE TIME:** 11 to 12 minutes | **YIELD:** 15 to 20 whoopie pies

A whoopie pie is like a mix of a cupcake and a filled soft cookie all in one. The story goes that these tasty treats were so good, all the kids would shout "Whoopie!" when they found one in their lunches. They also make the perfect treat to say thank you to your favorite teacher. These treats are a little sturdier than a cupcake for taking with you, and you can roll them in colored sprinkles for any celebration.

TOOLS/EQUIPMENT

- 1 or 2 baking sheets
- Parchment paper
- Electric mixer or stand mixer
- Wire cooling rack or kitchen towel
- Piping bag or strong plastic zip-top bag
- Cookie scoop (optional)

FOR THE WHOOPIE PIES

1 tablespoon fresh
  lemon juice
1 cup milk
½ cup (1 stick) unsalted
  butter, at room
  temperature
¾ cup brown sugar
¼ cup granulated sugar
1 large egg
1 teaspoon vanilla extract
2 cups all-purpose flour
⅔ cup unsweetened
  cocoa powder
1¼ teaspoons
  baking soda
1 teaspoon salt

PREHEAT THE OVEN TO 350°F.

Line the baking sheets with parchment paper.

MIX THE WET INGREDIENTS.

In a 1-cup measuring cup, add the lemon juice. Fill the measuring cup the rest of the way with milk and set aside for 5 to 10 minutes to make buttermilk. In a large mixing bowl with an electric mixer or in the bowl of a stand mixer, cream together ½ cup of butter, the brown sugar, and granulated sugar. In a small bowl, beat the egg with a fork and add it to the large bowl. Add 1 teaspoon of vanilla and the lemon-milk mixture and mix all the ingredients well until they are combined.

ADD THE DRY INGREDIENTS AND MAKE A BATTER.

In a medium bowl, combine the flour, cocoa, baking soda, and salt. Mix all the dry ingredients well, then add the dry ingredients to your wet ingredients and mix well until combined. The batter will be a little on the fudgy side.

FOR THE FILLING

½ cup (1 stick) unsalted butter, at room temperature
4 ounces cream cheese, at room temperature
2 cups powdered sugar
1 teaspoon vanilla extract
Sprinkles

Try Instead: Whoopie pies come in lots of other flavors—like pumpkin, chocolate, peanut butter, or even gingerbread. The fastest way to change the flavor is to roll the outside of the whoopie pies in candy cane bits, graham crackers, or other crushed-up candies.

BAKE YOUR WHOOPEE PIES.

Place 2 tablespoons of batter for each cookie on the prepared baking sheets. Try to keep your whoopie pies in as much of a circle and as even in size as you can. (A cookie scoop really helps to make the whoopie pies even, but most standard scoops are 1½ tablespoons. If you use a cookie scoop, expect to have a few more, slightly smaller whoopie pies!) Bake in the oven for 11 to 12 minutes. Remove quickly from the pan as soon as you can and let the whoopie pies cool on a wire rack or clean kitchen towel.

MIX THE CREAM CHEESE FILLING.

In a large mixing bowl with an electric mixer or in the bowl of a stand mixer, whip ½ cup of butter for 5 minutes. Scrape down the sides of the bowl, then add the cream cheese and beat for 1 to 2 minutes more. Scrape down the sides of the bowl and add the powdered sugar ½ cup at a time, mixing well between each addition. Add 1 teaspoon of vanilla and mix for 1 minute more.

MATCH YOUR WHOOPIE PIES TO ADD FILLING.

Match up your whoopie pies in pairs so that they are as close in size and shape as possible. Fill an icing bag or zip-top bag with filling (for easy bag-filling instructions, see page 19). Snip a medium hole in the end of your bag.

ADD THE FILLING TO THE WHOOPIE PIES.

On the flat side of one of your whoopie pies, pipe filling around the outside edge as close to the edge as possible, then swirl in, filling into the center. Place a second whoopie pie on top. Roll the edge in sprinkles to decorate.

School Spirit Sprinkle Cookies

PREP TIME: 20 minutes | **BAKE TIME:** 13 to 14 minutes | **YIELD:** 18 to 20 cookies

Cheer on your favorite team or just show off your school spirit with fun and festive sprinkled treats. No matter what school you go to or where you are, they can be customized with your school colors. Delicious and buttery, these cream cheese cookies are perfect for your next fundraiser, sporting event, picnic, or any school celebration.

TOOLS/EQUIPMENT

- 1 or 2 baking sheets
- Parchment paper
- Electric mixer or stand mixer (optional)

½ cup (1 stick) butter, at room temperature

4 ounces cream cheese, at room temperature

½ cup sugar

1 large egg

1 teaspoon vanilla extract

½ teaspoon salt

1½ cups all-purpose flour

4 to 5 ounces sprinkles in your school's colors

PREHEAT THE OVEN TO 350°F.

Line the baking sheets with parchment paper.

CREAM TOGETHER THE CREAM CHEESE, BUTTER, AND SUGAR.

In a large mixing bowl with a strong wooden spoon or an electric mixer or in the bowl of a stand mixer, cream together the butter and cream cheese until well mixed. Next, cream the sugar into the cream cheese mixture for an additional 1 to 2 minutes.

SEPARATE THE EGG AND MIX THE WET INGREDIENTS INTO THE DOUGH.

Separate the egg by cracking the egg over a small bowl, catching the egg yolk with the shell. Let the egg white drip into the bowl and put the egg yolk into a second bowl. (You can use the egg white for another use, like the Gooey Passover Double-Chocolate Flourless Cookies on page 36). Then add the egg yolk and vanilla to the cream cheese mixture and mix until creamy and smooth.

MIX THE DRY INGREDIENTS IN TO FORM A DOUGH.

Add the salt to the cream cheese mixture by sprinkling it around the bowl. Add the flour to the bowl and mix well. Put the dough in the refrigerator for 15 minutes to make it less sticky and easier to roll.

ROLL THE COOKIE DOUGH IN SPRINKLES AND BAKE.

Roll the cookie dough into 16 dough balls, about the same size as a ping-pong ball. Place the sprinkles in a small bowl. Roll each of the cookie dough balls in sprinkles and then place on the baking sheet about 1 inch apart.

BAKE THE COOKIES.

Bake the cookies for 13 to 14 minutes. Your cookies may be a little gooey inside, but they shouldn't be raw. They will firm up as they cool. Once they are cool enough, enjoy your cookies!

Bake Sale Chocolate Chip Shortbread Cookies

PREP TIME: 20 Minutes | **BAKE TIME:** 10 to 12 minutes | **YIELD:** 20 cookies

Choosing what treats to make and sell at your bake sale is tough. These chocolate chip shortbread cookies are buttery tasting, chocolatey, and can be packaged in little bags super easily. Along with being delicious, these treats don't have any dairy, gluten, or nuts, and they're vegan, so they're perfect for sharing with everyone!

TOOLS/EQUIPMENT
- 1 or 2 baking sheets
- Parchment paper
- Large clean drinking glass

1½ cups gluten-free flour
6 tablespoons sugar
½ teaspoon salt
¾ cup plus 1 tablespoon vegan buttery spread (such as Earth Balance), at room temperature
¾ cup allergy-friendly chocolate chips (such as Enjoy Life)

PREHEAT THE OVEN TO 350°F.
Line the baking sheets with parchment paper.

MIX THE DRY INGREDIENTS.
In a large bowl, mix together your flour, sugar, and salt until they are well combined.

ADD THE VEGAN BUTTER TO THE DOUGH.
Cut the flour mixture into your vegan buttery spread. The more you mix, the more the mixture will look and feel similar to damp sand. The dough should start to hold together when you press it between your fingers. Fold the chocolate chips into the dough gently. Chill your dough in the refrigerator for 10 to 15 minutes to help it firm up more.

ROLL THE COOKIES AND PRESS THEM FLATTER.
Roll the dough into 1-inch balls. Take the bottom of a clean drinking glass and gently press down on your dough balls to spread the cookies out.

BAKE THE COOKIES.
Bake your cookies for 10 to 12 minutes. The cookies will be a little crumbly, but delicious. These cookies continue to cook on the pan and firm up more as they cool.

Feeling Prickly Cactus Cupcakes

PREP TIME: 30 Minutes | **BAKE TIME:** 17 to 20 minutes | **YIELD:** 12 to 14 cupcakes

When someone is sick, they often feel a little prickly around the edges. Make them a plate of these fun cactus cupcakes that are both spiky and sweet—they are sure to brighten their day. These cupcakes are also a lot of fun for a summer party. Remember that cactuses usually don't have arms that match perfectly, so your cactus cupcakes don't have to be identical to be fun!

TOOLS/EQUIPMENT

- Muffin pan
- Cupcake liners
- Baking sheet
- Parchment paper
- Electric mixer or stand mixer
- Toothpick
- Wire cooling rack or kitchen towel
- Piping bags or strong plastic zip-top bags

FOR THE CUPCAKES

2 large eggs
¾ cup granulated sugar
½ cup yogurt
½ cup oil
2 teaspoons vanilla extract
1 cup all-purpose flour
½ cup unsweetened cocoa powder
1¼ teaspoons baking powder
½ teaspoon baking soda
½ teaspoon salt
2 tablespoons milk

PREHEAT THE OVEN TO 350°F.

Line the muffin pan with cupcake liners and a baking sheet with parchment paper.

MIX THE CUPCAKE BATTER.

In a large mixing bowl with a strong wooden spoon or an electric mixer, or in the bowl of a stand mixer, beat the eggs. Mix the granulated sugar, yogurt, oil, and 2 teaspoons of vanilla until combined. In a medium mixing bowl, add the flour, cocoa, baking powder, baking soda, and salt and mix until well combined. Add your flour and cocoa mixture to your wet ingredients and mix well. Then add 2 tablespoons of milk to thin your batter just a little.

BAKE THE CUPCAKES.

Fill each cupcake liner about two-thirds full with batter. Bake for 17 to 20 minutes, until a toothpick inserted in the center of a cupcake comes out clean with no batter clinging to it. Take the cupcakes out of the muffin pan when they're cool enough to handle and allow them to cool completely on a towel or wire rack.

› CONTINUED

FOR THE FROSTING AND DECORATIONS

2 cups green candy melts
White sprinkles
½ cup (1 stick) unsalted butter, at room temperature
2 cups powdered sugar
2 tablespoons milk
1 teaspoon vanilla extract
3 to 4 sheets of graham crackers

MELT THE CHOCOLATE FOR THE CACTUSES.

Melt the candy melts according to the package instructions, then pour it into a zip-top bag or piping bag using the method on page 19. Snip a small hole in the bag carefully—the chocolate can flow fast.

DRAW THE CACTUSES OUT OF CHOCOLATE.

Use the chocolate to draw a cactus on the parchment paper. Start by making the thicker center part of the cactus, then fill in and add arms. Your cactus should be 2 to 3 inches tall. Sprinkle on a few white sprinkles right away before the chocolate hardens. You need one cactus per cupcake, but make two or three extra, just in case any come out a little wonky.

PLACE THE PAN WITH THE CACTUSES IN THE FREEZER.

Place the entire pan in the freezer for at least 5 minutes. This causes the chocolate to harden more firmly.

MAKE THE FROSTING.

In a clean large mixing bowl with an electric mixer or in the clean bowl of a stand mixer, beat the butter on medium speed for 5 minutes. The butter will turn a paler color. Scrape down the sides of the bowl. Next, slowly add the powdered sugar, ½ cup at a time. Mix on low, then medium speed, until all the sugar is well mixed into the butter. Add 2 tablespoons of milk and 1 teaspoon of vanilla and mix for 1 to 2 minutes.

Feeling Prickly
Cactus Cupcakes,
page 151

FROST AND DECORATE THE CUPCAKES.

In a zip-top bag, crush the graham crackers, then pour them in a small bowl. Using a spatula, frost the tops of your cupcakes with a thin layer of frosting, then dip the cupcake in graham cracker crumbs. Repeat for all the cupcakes. Remove the cactuses from the freezer and add a cactus to the top of each cupcake.

Helpful Hint: You can draw cactuses on a piece of paper with a permanent marker and slide it under your parchment paper to give yourself a template (like in the Shark Attack Cheesecakes on page 65).

Caramel and Pretzel Cookies

PREP TIME: 20 minutes | **BAKE TIME:** 10 to 11 minutes | **YIELD:** 20 to 22 cookies

Have someone to say thanks to? A friend, a teacher, a parent, or a coach, maybe? No matter who it is, a batch of caramel, chocolate, and pretzel cookies will do the trick—they're the perfect sweet-and-salty combo, so they'll please almost anyone. The salt in the pretzels pulls out the sweet flavors, but you can also experiment with a tiny sprinkle of salt on the caramel at the end.

TOOLS/EQUIPMENT

- 1 or 2 baking sheets
- Parchment paper
- Clean kitchen scissors
- Electric mixer or stand mixer (optional)
- Cookie scoop (optional)

18 to 20 soft caramel candies
½ cup (1 stick) unsalted butter, at room temperature
½ cup brown sugar
¼ cup granulated sugar
1 large egg
1 teaspoon vanilla extract
1½ cups all-purpose flour
½ teaspoon baking soda
½ teaspoon salt
½ cup chocolate chips
½ cup pretzel pieces

PREHEAT THE OVEN TO 350°F.

Line the baking sheets with parchment paper. Unwrap all of the caramel candies, cut each one into 4 pieces with clean kitchen scissors, and put the pieces in a small bowl.

MIX THE WET INGREDIENTS TOGETHER.

In a large mixing bowl with a strong wooden spoon or electric mixer or in the bowl of a stand mixer, cream together the butter, brown sugar, and granulated sugar until there are no more chunks of butter. Add the egg and vanilla, mixing together until smooth.

MIX THE DRY INGREDIENTS AND MAKE A DOUGH.

In a medium mixing bowl, combine the flour, baking soda, and salt, then mix well until combined. Add the flour mixture to the wet ingredients, then mix until the dough is thick like Play-Doh.

FOLD THE CHOCOLATE AND PRETZELS INTO THE COOKIE DOUGH.

Fold the chocolate chips and pretzel pieces into your dough gently with a spatula or spoon.

› CONTINUED

Trouble-shooting: Don't use an electric mixer to fold the pretzels into the batter—use a spatula or spoon. The mixer will crush the pretzels too much and your cookies will be missing crunch!

BAKE THE COOKIES IN THE OVEN.

Using a cookie scoop or a tablespoon, scoop out 2 tablespoons of dough and roll into a ball. Place 6 balls of dough on each baking sheet, leaving about 2 inches between each, and bake for 10 to 11 minutes, until gooey but not raw.

ADD CARAMEL TO THE COOKIES.

Remove the cookies from the oven and place the pan on a pot holder. While the cookies are still warm on the pan, add 3 or 4 caramel pieces to each cookie by gently pressing them in. Work fast while the cookies are still hot. You can also press a few extra chocolate chips or pretzel bits into the top of the cookies to make them look more amazing!

Caramel and
Pretzel Cookies,
page 155

Nuts about You Anniversary Cookies

PREP TIME: 20 minutes | **BAKE TIME:** 10 to 11 minutes | **YIELD:** 16 to 18 cookies

Have you ever been to a wedding? Maybe you were a ring bearer or flower girl. Weddings are usually a happy party celebrating two people falling in love. Many people celebrate that love every year, and you can, too! Make these yummy peanut butter and chocolate cookies—it's one little way to say "I love you guys, too!"

TOOLS/EQUIPMENT

- 1 or 2 baking sheets
- Parchment paper
- Whisk (optional)
- Cookie scoop (optional)
- Wire cooling rack or kitchen towel

1 large egg

½ cup sugar

Oil or cooking oil spray, for greasing the measuring cup

1 cup peanut butter

⅔ cup chocolate candies (like M&M's)

⅓ cup salted peanuts

PREHEAT THE OVEN TO 350°F.
Line the baking sheets with parchment paper.

MIX THE WET INGREDIENTS FOR YOUR COOKIE DOUGH.
In a large mixing bowl, crack the egg and beat it with a fork or whisk. Add the sugar to the bowl and mix well.

MIX THE DRY INGREDIENTS AND MAKE THE COOKIE DOUGH.
Spray your measuring cup with a little oil to keep things from sticking and then measure your peanut butter. Mix the peanut butter with the egg and sugar to make a dough.

FOLD IN THE CHOCOLATE AND PEANUTS.
Fold the chocolate candies and the peanuts into the dough. Stir well until combined, then chill the dough in the freezer for 10 minutes.

SCOOP THE COOKIE DOUGH ONTO THE PAN.
Using a cookie scoop or a tablespoon, scoop out 2 tablespoons of dough and roll into a ball. Gently flatten the dough balls a little with your hand. You can also add a few extra chocolate pieces on top of your dough before you bake the cookies to make them look fancier.

BAKE AND COOL THE COOKIES.

Place 8 dough balls on each baking sheet and bake for 10 to 11 minutes, until gooey but not raw. Allow the cookies to cool for 2 to 3 minutes on the pan, then move the cookies to a wire rack or clean kitchen towel. The cookies will continue to become a little crunchier as they cool. Enjoy!

Did You Know? It takes 540 peanuts to make one 12-ounce jar of peanut butter. That's a lot of peanuts!

Peanut Butter and
Pumpkin Pup Cookies,
page 161

Peanut Butter and Pumpkin Pup Cookies

PREP TIME: 15 minutes | **BAKE TIME:** 10 to 12 minutes | **YIELD:** 12 to 16 cookies

Not all holidays are for humans! Celebrate your pup's adoption or birthday (or them just being a good boy or girl) with these delicious homemade treats your dog will love!

TOOLS/EQUIPMENT

- 2 baking sheets
- Parchment paper
- Blender or food processor
- Rolling pin
- 2- to 3-inch bone-shaped cookie cutter
- Wire cooling rack or kitchen towel

1¼ cups oats, divided

½ cup plus 1 tablespoon canned pumpkin (just pumpkin)

½ cup peanut butter (just peanuts)

Did You Know?
Peanut butter is generally safe for dogs—as long as it's just peanut butter. Some brands can have alternative sweeteners, and one called xylitol can be dangerous for pups.

PREHEAT YOUR OVEN TO 350°F.
Line the baking sheets with parchment paper.

MAKE OAT FLOUR BY PULSING IN THE BLENDER.
In a blender or food processor, blitz your oats a few times until they become a powder. This turns the oats into oat flour.

MIX THE DOUGH FOR THE COOKIES.
Add 1 cup of your oat flour to your mixing bowl. Next add your pumpkin and peanut butter and mix well until the mixture becomes a thick dough that feels a little grainy.

ROLL THE DOUGH AND CUT THE COOKIES.
Add ¼ cup of oat flour to a clean work surface. Roll your dough to about ¼ inch in thickness. Use a bone-shaped cookie cutter to cut out the treats, or you can roll the dough into dough balls with a tablespoon of dough each. Press the dough ball down with a fork one direction, and then the other direction, making a tic-tac-toe board on the cookie to flatten it.

BAKE THE COOKIES.
Bake the cookies for 10 to 12 minutes, or until they are firm. It's OK to bake them longer so they're extra crunchy.

COOL THE COOKIES.
Cool your cookies on a towel or wire rack for at least 15 minutes before giving the treat to your dog.

MEASUREMENT CONVERSIONS

Volume Equivalents (Liquid)

US STANDARD	US STANDARD (OUNCES)	METRIC (APPROXIMATE)
2 tablespoons	1 fl. oz.	30 mL
¼ cup	2 fl. oz.	60 mL
½ cup	4 fl. oz.	120 mL
1 cup	8 fl. oz.	240 mL
1½ cups	12 fl. oz.	355 mL
2 cups or 1 pint	16 fl. oz.	475 mL
4 cups or 1 quart	32 fl. oz.	1 L
1 gallon	128 fl. oz.	4 L

Oven Temperatures

FAHRENHEIT (F)	CELSIUS (C) (APPROXIMATE)
250°F	120°C
300°F	150°C
325°F	165°C
350°F	180°C
375°F	190°C
400°F	200°C
425°F	220°C
450°F	230°C

Volume Equivalents (Dry)

US STANDARD	METRIC (APPROXIMATE)
⅛ teaspoon	0.5 mL
¼ teaspoon	1 mL
½ teaspoon	2 mL
¾ teaspoon	4 mL
1 teaspoon	5 mL
1 tablespoon	15 mL
¼ cup	59 mL
⅓ cup	79 mL
½ cup	118 mL
⅔ cup	156 mL
¾ cup	177 mL
1 cup	235 mL
2 cups or 1 pint	475 mL
3 cups	700 mL
4 cups or 1 quart	1 L

Weight Equivalents

US STANDARD	METRIC (APPROXIMATE)
½ ounce	15 g
1 ounce	30 g
2 ounces	60 g
4 ounces	115 g
8 ounces	225 g
12 ounces	340 g
16 ounces or 1 pound	455 g

INDEX

·················

A

Allergens, 25
Apples
    Apple Crisp Pizza
        Party, 97–98
    Caramel Apple
        Blondies, 102–103
April Fools' Tostada
    Cookies, 33–35

B

Bake Sale Chocolate Chip
    Shortbread Cookies, 150
Baking mats, 6
Baking pans and sheets, 5–6
Baking powder, 9, 11
Baking soda, 9, 11
Bars. *See also* Brownies
    Caramel Apple
        Blondies, 102–103
    Super Bowl Football Field
        Cookie Bars, 132–134
Beating, 15
Berries
    Bursting Blueberry Mini
        Galettes (Pies!), 77–78
    Chewy Cranberry, Oatmeal,
        and White Chocolate
        Chip Cookies, 110–111
    Cool Strawberry and
        Chocolate Icebox
        Cake, 75–76
    Raspberry and Cream
        Cheese Cupcakes, 39–40
    Raspberry Sweetheart
        Rolls, 137–138
    Ultimate Memorial Day
        Pound Cake, 56–57
    Watermelon Pizza Cookie
        Cake, 73–74
The Biggest Cinnamon-Sugar
    Christmas Donut
    Ever, 120–121

Birthday candles, 12
Blooming Brownies, 46–47
Brownies
    Blooming Brownies, 46–47
    Brownie à la Mode
        Cupcakes, 68–69
    Mermaid Brownie
        Pops, 61–62
    Trick-or-Treat
        Candy Overload
        Brownies, 86–87
Bursting Blueberry Mini
    Galettes (Pies!), 77–78
Butter, 10, 11

C

Cakes. *See also* Cupcakes
    The Biggest
        Cinnamon-Sugar
        Christmas Donut
        Ever, 120–121
    Choco-Vanilla Birthday
        Cake, 143–145
    Cool Strawberry and
        Chocolate Icebox
        Cake, 75–76
    Let It Snow! Snowman
        Cake, 127–129
    Ultimate Memorial Day
        Pound Cake, 56–57
    Watermelon Pizza Cookie
        Cake, 73–74
    World Series All-Star
        Pull-Apart Cake, 71–72
Camping Party S'mores
    Cookies, 63–64
Candies, 12
Candy Corn Magic Cookies, 91
Candy eyes, 12
Candy melts, 12
Caramel and Pretzel
    Cookies, 155–156

Caramel Apple
    Blondies, 102–103
Changing Leaves
    Snickerdoodles,
    104–105
Cheesecakes, Shark
    Attack, 65–66
Chewy Cranberry, Oatmeal,
    and White Chocolate Chip
    Cookies, 110–111
Chocolate. *See also* White
    chocolate
    April Fools' Tostada
        Cookies, 33–35
    Bake Sale Chocolate Chip
        Shortbread Cookies, 150
    Blooming Brownies, 46–47
    Brownie à la Mode
        Cupcakes, 68–69
    Camping Party S'mores
        Cookies, 63–64
    Candies, 12
    Caramel and Pretzel
        Cookies, 155–156
    Chips, 9
    Chocolate Chip and
        Almond Spanish
        Polvorones, 118–119
    Chocolate-Cinnamon
        Rugelach
        Cookies, 130–131
    Chocolate-Peppermint
        Crinkle
        Cookies, 125–126
    Choco-Vanilla Birthday
        Cake, 143–145
    Cool Strawberry and
        Chocolate Icebox
        Cake, 75–76
Chocolate (*continued*)
    Day of the Dead Sugar Skull
        Cookies, 92–94

Easter Chick Surprise!
Cupcakes, 30–31
Feeling Prickly Cactus
Cupcakes, 151–154
Fudgy Diwali Chocolate
Burfi, 95–96
Gooey Passover
Double-Chocolate
Flourless
Cookies, 36–37
Mermaid Brownie
Pops, 61–62
Nuts about You Anniversary
Cookies, 158–159
Spooky Ghost
Double-Chocolate
Cupcakes, 82–84
Super Bowl Football
Field Cookie
Bars, 132–134
Trick-or-Treat
Candy Overload
Brownies, 86–87
Ultimate Fiesta
Chocolate Churro
Cups, 43–44
Watermelon Pizza Cookie
Cake, 73–74
"Whoopie! Thanks for
Being My Teacher"
Pies, 146–147
"You're a Smart
Cookie" Graduation
Cookies, 52–53
Choco-Vanilla Birthday
Cake, 143–145
Chopping, 17
Christmas Cutout
Cookies, 122–123
Cleaning up, 3
Cocoa powder, 10
Coconut
April Fools' Tostada
Cookies, 33–35
Cookie cutters, 7
Cookie scoops, 7
Cookies. *See also* Bars
April Fools' Tostada
Cookies, 33–35

Bake Sale Chocolate Chip
Shortbread Cookies, 150
Camping Party S'mores
Cookies, 63–64
Candy Corn Magic
Cookies, 91
Caramel and Pretzel
Cookies, 155–156
Changing Leaves
Snickerdoodles,
104–105
Chewy Cranberry, Oatmeal,
and White Chocolate
Chip Cookies, 110–111
Chocolate Chip and
Almond Spanish
Polvorones, 118–119
Chocolate-Cinnamon
Rugelach
Cookies, 130–131
Chocolate-Peppermint
Crinkle
Cookies, 125–126
Christmas Cutout
Cookies, 122–123
Day of the Dead Sugar Skull
Cookies, 92–94
Eid Moon Cookies, 49–51
Gooey Passover
Double-Chocolate
Flourless
Cookies, 36–37
Lemonade Bunny
Thumbprint
Cookies, 28–29
Lunar New Year
Walnut
Cookies, 135–136
Nuts about You Anniversary
Cookies, 158–159
School Spirit Sprinkle
Cookies, 148–149
Stained Glass Cookie
Ornaments, 115–117
Sweet Orange and
White Chocolate
Cookies, 112–113

Sweet Orange
Hamantaschen (Hat)
Cookies, 41–42
Watermelon Pizza Cookie
Cake, 73–74
"Whoopie! Thanks for
Being My Teacher"
Pies, 146–147
"You're a Smart
Cookie" Graduation
Cookies, 52–53
Cool Strawberry and Chocolate
Icebox Cake, 75–76
Cream, 9
Cooling racks, 7
Cream cheese, 12
Choco-Vanilla Birthday
Cake, 143–145
Let It Snow! Snowman
Cake, 127–129
Raspberry and Cream
Cheese Cupcakes, 39–40
School Spirit Sprinkle
Cookies, 148–149
Shark Attack
Cheesecakes, 65–66
Spooky Ghost
Double-Chocolate
Cupcakes, 82–84
Super Bowl Football Field
Cookie Bars, 132–134
Trick-or-Treat
Candy Overload
Brownies, 86–87
Watermelon Pizza Cookie
Cake, 73–74
"Whoopie! Thanks for
Being My Teacher"
Pies, 146–147
World Series All-Star
Pull-Apart
Cake, 71–72
Creaming, 15
Cupcakes
Brownie à la Mode
Cupcakes, 68–69
Easter Chick Surprise!
Cupcakes, 30–31

Feeling Prickly Cactus
        Cupcakes, 151–154
Raspberry and Cream
        Cheese Cupcakes, 39–40
Red, White, and Blue Emoji
        Cupcakes, 59–60
Spooky Ghost
        Double-Chocolate
        Cupcakes, 82–84
World Series All-Star
        Pull-Apart
        Cake, 71–72
Cutting in, 16

D
Dairy substitutions, 25
Day of the Dead Sugar Skull
        Cookies, 92–94
Decorations, 12
Dog treats
        Peanut Butter and Pumpkin
        Pup Cookies, 161

E
Easter Chick Surprise!
        Cupcakes, 30–31
Eggs, 9, 11
Eid Moon Cookies, 49–51
Electric mixers, 6
Equipment, 4–7

F
Feeling Prickly Cactus
        Cupcakes, 151–154
Flour, 9
Folding, 16
Food allergies, 25
Food coloring, 12
Frosting, 18–19
Fudgy Diwali Chocolate
        Burfi, 95–96

G
Gifting treats, 23
Glazes, 18
Gluten, 25
Gooey Passover
        Double-Chocolate
        Flourless Cookies, 36–37

Graham crackers, 25
        Camping Party S'mores
        Cookies, 63–64
        Cool Strawberry and
        Chocolate Icebox
        Cake, 75–76
        Feeling Prickly Cactus
        Cupcakes, 151–154
        Shark Attack
        Cheesecakes, 65–66
Grapes
        Watermelon Pizza Cookie
        Cake, 73–74
Grating, 17

H
High-altitude, 20

I
Ice cream
        Brownie à la Mode
        Cupcakes, 68–69
Icings, 18
Ingredients
        measuring dry, 14
        measuring wet, 13
        staples, 9–10

J
Jam
        Raspberry
        Sweetheart Rolls,
        137–138
        Shark Attack
        Cheesecakes, 65–66
        Sweet Orange
        Hamantaschen (Hat)
        Cookies, 41–42

K
Knife skills, 17

L
Lemonade Bunny Thumbprint
        Cookies, 28–29
Let It Snow! Snowman
        Cake, 127–129
Liquids, 11

Lunar New Year Walnut
        Cookies, 135–136

M
Marshmallows, 12
        Blooming
        Brownies, 46–47
        Camping Party S'mores
        Cookies, 63–64
        Spooky Ghost
        Double-Chocolate
        Cupcakes, 82–84
Measuring, 13–14
Measuring cups and
        spoons, 4–5
Mermaid Brownie Pops, 61–62
Milk, 9
Mixers, 6, 7
Mixing, 15–16
Mixing bowls, 4
Muffins, Ooey-Gooey
        Maple-Cinnamon French
        Toast, 100–101

N
Nut-free
        Apple Crisp Pizza
        Party, 97–98
        April Fools' Tostada
        Cookies, 33–35
        Bake Sale Chocolate Chip
        Shortbread Cookies, 150
        The Biggest
        Cinnamon-Sugar
        Christmas Donut
        Ever, 120–121
        Blooming
        Brownies, 46–47
        Brownie à la Mode
        Cupcakes, 68–69
Nut-free (continued)
        Bursting Blueberry Mini
        Galettes (Pies!), 77–78
        Camping Party S'mores
        Cookies, 63–64
        Candy Corn Magic
        Cookies, 91
        Caramel and Pretzel
        Cookies, 155–156

Caramel Apple
Blondies, 102–103
Changing Leaves
Snickerdoodles,
104–105
Chewy Cranberry, Oatmeal,
and White Chocolate
Chip Cookies, 110–111
Chocolate-Cinnamon
Rugelach
Cookies, 130–131
Chocolate-Peppermint
Crinkle
Cookies, 125–126
Choco-Vanilla Birthday
Cake, 143–145
Christmas Cutout
Cookies, 122–123
Cool Strawberry and
Chocolate Icebox
Cake, 75–76
Day of the Dead Sugar Skull
Cookies, 92–94
Easter Chick Surprise!
Cupcakes, 30–31
Eid Moon Cookies, 49–51
Feeling Prickly Cactus
Cupcakes, 151–154
Gooey Passover
Double-Chocolate
Flourless
Cookies, 36–37
Lemonade Bunny
Thumbprint
Cookies, 28–29
Let It Snow! Snowman
Cake, 127–129
Mermaid Brownie
Pops, 61–62
Ooey-Gooey
Maple-Cinnamon
French Toast
Muffins, 100–101
Peanut Butter and Pumpkin
Pup Cookies, 161
Pumpkin Pie
Dumplings, 88–89
Raspberry and Cream
Cheese Cupcakes, 39–40

Raspberry Sweetheart
Rolls, 137–138
Red, White, and Blue Emoji
Cupcakes, 59–60
School Spirit Sprinkle
Cookies, 148–149
Shark Attack
Cheesecakes, 65–66
Spooky Ghost
Double-Chocolate
Cupcakes, 82–84
Stained Glass Cookie
Ornaments, 115–117
Super Bowl Football Field
Cookie Bars, 132–134
Sweet Orange and
White Chocolate
Cookies, 112–113
Sweet Orange
Hamantaschen (Hat)
Cookies, 41–42
Trick-or-Treat
Candy Overload
Brownies, 86–87
Ultimate Fiesta Chocolate
Churro Cups, 43–44
Ultimate Memorial Day
Pound Cake, 56–57
Watermelon Pizza Cookie
Cake, 73–74
"Whoopie! Thanks for
Being My Teacher"
Pies, 146–147
World Series All-Star
Pull-Apart
Cake, 71–72
"You're a Smart
Cookie" Graduation
Cookies, 52–53
Nuts
Chocolate Chip and
Almond Spanish
Polvorones, 118–119
Fudgy Diwali Chocolate
Burfi, 95–96
Gooey Passover
Double-Chocolate
Flourless
Cookies, 36–37

Lunar New Year Walnut
Cookies, 135–136
Nuts about You Anniversary
Cookies, 158–159

O
Oats
Apple Crisp Pizza
Party, 97–98
Chewy Cranberry, Oatmeal,
and White Chocolate
Chip Cookies, 110–111
Peanut Butter and
Pumpkin Pup
Cookies, 161
Ooey-Gooey Maple-Cinnamon
French Toast
Muffins, 100–101
Oranges
Sweet Orange and
White Chocolate
Cookies, 112–113
Sweet Orange
Hamantaschen (Hat)
Cookies, 41–42
Oven mitts, 4
Oven safety, 8

P
Parchment paper, 6
Pastries
Apple Crisp Pizza
Party, 97–98
Pastries (continued)
Pumpkin Pie
Dumplings, 88–89
Raspberry
Sweetheart
Rolls, 137–138
Ultimate Fiesta
Chocolate Churro
Cups, 43–44
Peanut butter
Nuts about You Anniversary
Cookies, 158–159
Peanut Butter and
Pumpkin Pup
Cookies, 161
Pies

Bursting Blueberry Mini
    Galettes (Pies!), 77–78
Piping, 18–19
Pot holders, 4
Preparing to
    bake, 2–3
Pretzel and Caramel
    Cookies, 155–156
Pumpkin
    Peanut Butter and
        Pumpkin Pup
        Cookies, 161
    Pumpkin Pie
        Dumplings, 88–89

R
Raspberry and Cream Cheese
    Cupcakes, 39–40
Raspberry Sweetheart
    Rolls, 137–138
Recipes, about, 24
Red, White, and Blue Emoji
    Cupcakes, 59–60
Rolling pins, 7
Rules, 2–3

S
Safety
    kitchen, 3
    knife, 17
    oven, 8
Salt, 10, 11
School Spirit
    Sprinkle Cookies, 148–149
Science of
    baking, 11
Shark Attack
    Cheesecakes, 65–66
Shredding, 17
Slicing, 17
Spatulas, 4

Spooky Ghost
    Double-Chocolate
        Cupcakes, 82–84
Sprinkles, 10
Stained Glass
    Cookie
        Ornaments, 115–117
Stand mixers, 7
Stirring, 16
Substitutions, 25
Sugar, 10
Super Bowl Football
    Field Cookie
        Bars, 132–134
Sweet Orange and
    White Chocolate
        Cookies, 112–113
Sweet Orange Hamantaschen
    (Hat) Cookies, 41–42

T
Tools, 4–7
Trick-or-Treat Candy Overload
    Brownies, 86–87
Troubleshooting, 21–22

U
Ultimate Fiesta Chocolate
    Churro Cups, 43–44
Ultimate Memorial Day Pound
    Cake, 56–57

V
Vanilla extract, 10

W
Watermelon Pizza Cookie
    Cake, 73–74
Whipping, 15
Whisks, 4
White chocolate
    Brownie à la Mode
        Cupcakes, 68–69

Candy Corn Magic
    Cookies, 91
Chewy Cranberry, Oatmeal,
    and White Chocolate
        Chip Cookies, 110–111
Mermaid Brownie
    Pops, 61–62
Sweet Orange and
    White Chocolate
        Cookies, 112–113
"Whoopie! Thanks for
    Being My Teacher"
        Pies, 146–147
World Series All-Star
    Pull-Apart
        Cake, 71–72

Y
"You're a Smart Cookie"
    Graduation
        Cookies, 52–53

Z
Zesting, 18

ACKNOWLEDGMENTS

Thank you to my husband, Noel, who cheered me on and supported me every step of the way. I couldn't have made this book without your love and support—and taste testing! Thanks for being my number one fan always and for helping me be brave.

Thank you to my daughter, Hailey, the number one kid taste tester. Your excitement is the reason the recipes in this book come alive. I can't wait to see what you create next.

To my parents, Lisa and Paul, thank you for encouraging me to push myself to learn more every day, for your love and sense of humor.

To my brother, Matt, thanks for your encouragement and laughs that always make celebrating more fun.

To the team at Callisto, thank you for the encouragement to create magic together and allowing me to create for so many kids and families in the kitchen.

ABOUT THE AUTHOR

Kristy Richardson is the founder of the popular website OnMyKidsPlate.com. She shares fresh and fun recipes for families and kids and tons of ideas for parents. On her website and channels, you'll find fun sweets and snacks, tasty dinner ideas, and lunchbox inspiration. Kristy brings a creativity to food that is fast, fun, fresh, and tasty for the whole family.

Her work has been featured on 13ABC, WTOL, *The Toledo Blade*, BuzzFeed, Brit + Co, and the Feedfeed.

She currently lives in Prescott, Arizona, with her husband, Noel, and eight-year-old daughter, Hailey. She is originally from Columbus, Ohio, but has moved with her family several times.

Follow her on social media for more great recipes and ideas on Instagram, Facebook, and Pinterest @OnMyKidsPlate.

Printed in the USA
CPSIA information can be obtained
at www.ICGtesting.com
LVHW081656301123
764704LV00004B/55